ARE WE THERE YET?

Pilgrimage in the Season of Lent

© 2017 Forward Movement

All Rights Reserved.

Printed in the USA

ISBN 978-0-88028-442-4

Forward Movement

inspire disciples. empower evangelists.

ARE WE THERE YET?

Pilgrimage in the Season of Lent

Meditations by

Nancy Hopkins-Greene, Bo Cox, Jeffrey Queen,
Catherine Meeks, Teresa Pasquale Mateus,
Frank and Victoria Logue, Minda Cox

Introduction by Marek Zabriskie

Forward Movement

Cincinnati, Ohio

Contents

Are We There Yet?

Foreword

Since the day we left Eden, the people of God have been trying to make our way back to the place we most deeply belong—to the literal dust of our making and the unfathomably deep heart of God. The travels and travails we witness throughout the Bible and see most clearly in the life of Jesus bring to mind a quote from spiritual activist and writer Ram Dass: "We're all just walking each other home." And so it is with the idea of pilgrimage. Whether we are following the yellow arrows that mark the *Camino*, the white blazes that wend their way from Alabama to Maine on the Appalachian Trail, or simply obeying the sighs and signs of the Holy Spirit's leading, somewhere along our journey we will wonder, "Are we there yet?" Like God whispering to Elijah on the mountain, we will eventually come to realize that the journey—the wrestling and the wandering—is the real flesh and blood of our endeavor.

Pilgrims come in all shapes and sizes, as do the journeys we set for ourselves. The bald fact of pilgrimage is this: The furthest distance we will travel is the eighteen inches between our brains and our hearts. Every pilgrim is radically changed by the experience. We analyze our personal theologies, relationships, and habits—and even our relationship to time itself. The pilgrims who have contributed to this Lenten devotional share this truth of transformation in the stories of their journeys.

Whether you are planning a trip of your own or traveling through your memories and life experiences during this holy season, we invite you to join us as we make our way toward Jerusalem with Jesus. On the way, we will walk the *Camino* in Spain, visit Marian shrines in England and Wisconsin, bear witness to the pain of historic lynching sites in the American South, be reunited with beloved family members in India, hold hands around a prayer circle in a mental hospital, and scale Appalachian peaks. Through our journeys, may we be open to the miracles of love and life and awestruck by the One who is both our journey and our destination.

With prayers for a holy Lent,

Rachel Jones
Associate Editor, Forward Movement

Introduction
Wandering and Welcome

Now the LORD said to Abram, "Go from your country and your kindred and your father's house to the land that I will show you. I will make of you a great nation, and I will bless you, and make your name great, so that you will be a blessing. I will bless those who bless you, and the one who curses you I will curse; and in you all the families of the earth shall be blessed."

Genesis 12:1-3

The Journey

In 2013, I walked the *Camino Frances* (the French Way) as part a sabbatical. The *Camino de Santiago* (the Way of Saint James) is an ancient route leading to the cathedral city of Santiago, Spain, the legendary resting place of the relics of James the Greater (one of the sons of Zebedee). The *Camino Frances* begins in France and links up with the Spanish portion of the road just over the Pyrenees Mountains.   *Marek Zabriskie*

Wandering and Welcome

The pilgrim's path is a journey that transforms our inner being through hospitality, holy places, and the holy bearers of God's grace we meet along the way.

There are places of holiness all over the earth where humans have experienced the presence of God. When we travel to them, we become pilgrims. We are absorbed into the holiness of these places, and we are transformed by these liminal sites. Pilgrimage plays a major role in most of the world's major religions. Jews travel around the world to set foot on Mount Moriah. Muslims are required to make at least one hajj to Mecca. Hindus travel to Varanasi and Benares. Buddhists trek across the Himalayas to the holy city of Lhasa, Tibet. Christians journey to Jerusalem, Rome, Ephesus, Lourdes, Canterbury, Fatima, Mexico City, Walsingham, and Chimayo, among other pilgrimage sites.

Pilgrims challenge their minds and bodies to go beyond comfortable boundaries and familiar settings, making arduous trips across land and sea, trekking through forests, traversing rivers and ascending hills, drawn toward the spiritual energy of holy sites. The lives they live on their journey are transformed by prayer and learning, evenings shared with old and new friends, the formation of deep relationships, and countless moments of grace. Pilgrims walk in the open air, exposed to the elements, and they enjoy simple gifts like a good meal eaten with fellow travelers. Forests, fields, and watersheds become lifelong bosom friends, and the creative heart of God is revealed in the confluence of earth, air, and water. Pilgrims learn, as did that famous walker Saint Francis, that every bird has a sermon to sing to the glory of God.

During the Middle Ages, Christians made pilgrimage primarily to three sites: Jerusalem, Rome, and Santiago. Today, those sites are still popular places to journey, but in a world of easy travel, other sites have also become holy destinations— from Sepphoris to Sheboygan. The idea of pilgrimage has always been part of the Christian experience, since the earliest days of retracing Jesus' last steps on the *Via Dolorosa*. Since the dawn of affordable air travel and the booming tourist business, the idea of physical pilgrimage has become a more realistic discipline for many of the faithful.

My journey along the *Camino* altered how I lead my life, see things around me, and carry out my ministry. Walking the *Camino* taught me the value of moving through life at a slower pace. I was blessed to share great conversations with many people who may never darken the door of a church but have a strong spiritual capacity. I came to understand how little we need to be deeply satisfied and joyful.

More than anything else, walking the *Camino* taught me that everyone is on a journey, and each journey is different. Every person we meet along our journey has gifts to offer us, if we will keep our eyes and ears open and receptive. Likewise, we have something to offer to every person we meet, if we are willing to listen and be kind.

Teach us, O Lord, not to hold onto life too tightly, but lightly, gently, and gracefully. Teach us that significance and meaning in life come from the conversations we share along the journey with fellow travelers. Teach us to walk as pilgrims, traveling by faith, being open to surprise, receiving the gifts that you and others seek to offer us along the way. Transform and transfigure us as we travel. **Amen.**

The Week of Ash Wednesday
Purgation and Penance

The LORD is full of compassion and mercy, slow to anger and of great kindness. He will not always accuse us, nor will he keep his anger for ever. He has not dealt with us according to our sins, nor rewarded us according to our wickedness. For as the heavens are high above the earth, so is his mercy great upon those who fear him. As far as the east is from the west, so far has he removed our sins from us. As a father cares for his children, so does the LORD care for those who fear him. For he himself knows whereof we are made; he remembers that we are but dust. Our days are like the grass; we flourish like a flower of the field; when the wind goes over it, it is gone, and its place shall know it no more. But the merciful goodness of the LORD endures for ever on those who fear him, and his righteousness on children's children.

Psalm 103:8-17

The Journey

My husband Roger and I walked the centuries-old pilgrimage route of the *Camino de Santiago* in the spring of 2015. We followed the *Camino Frances*, beginning in St. Jean Pied-de-Port, France, and ending at the Cathedral of Santiago de Compostela, the alleged burial place of Saint James the Apostle. We had talked for years about doing this pilgrimage, and our empty nest finally made it possible. We had a remarkable journey, and we continue to process and appropriate its lessons in our lives. Among those lessons are the joy of traveling lightly, the importance of fellow pilgrims, and the fact that life is about the journey—not the destination.

Nancy Hopkins-Greene

Are We There Yet?

Ash Wednesday

We read numerous guidebooks and memoirs about the *Camino* and combed lists of what to bring. We spent hours in a local camping store buying clothes and gear, choosing hiking boots, finding and fitting backpacks.

Although both of us were in good shape, we were not experienced backpackers. But by the time we arrived in St. Jean Pied-de-Port, the starting place of our journey, we were feeling pretty good about ourselves. We had navigated our way by plane, train, and taxi. Surprising myself, I had even kept a conversation going in Spanish with the taxi driver on the trip from Pamplona. We found the place to obtain our pilgrim's passports and tied scallop shells—one of the traditional symbols of *Camino* pilgrims—to the back of our packs. Confident and ready, we set off on the *Camino*…and promptly got lost.

Truth is, with yellow arrows marking the way, it's not easy to get lost on the *Camino*. But somehow we managed it—walking a couple of miles in the wrong direction before realizing our mistake, turning back, and finally heading on the correct road over the Pyrenees. I suppose it was good to have this humbling experience so early in our pilgrimage.

One definition of the word repent is to turn around—to turn away from sin, to go in a different direction. As we began our pilgrimage, we literally and figuratively turned around. We needed to be reminded that we were not perfect or perfectly in control or even all that competent. We needed to recognize that we were—and are—simply human.

God remembers that we are *but dust*. These words of the psalm echo God's address to Adam and Eve as they are being expelled from the garden. "You are dust and to dust you shall return" (Genesis 3:19b). Earlier in the narrative, God picks up dirt—dust—and forms the first human. This Adam (literally "earth creature") is naked, vulnerable, made in the image of God but dependent on God for his very life. God breathes the breath of life into these dusty nostrils.

Every year on Ash Wednesday, we participate in a strange ritual—smearing ashes on our foreheads, reminding each other that we too are mortal beings, creatures of the earth, nothing more and nothing less. And we remember that we are radically dependent on the One who formed us and who continues to breathe life into and through us.

We have a tendency to hear these words about dust as punishment, as if God is trying to take us down a peg or two, dropping us like a cigarette butt onto the pavement, grinding the ash into the ground with the bottom of a shoe. Lent is

Are We There Yet?

sometimes understood as a time to skulk around in sackcloth and ashes, loudly repenting of our sins, making ourselves miserable by giving up things we love, praying that God will make us worthy of salvation.

But what if Lent is not primarily about sin and repentance but is a deep call to remember our creatureliness and our radical dependence on God? We are simply human. And one of our greatest sins is the sin of forgetting—forgetting that this earthly creature is really who we are. We play God in trying to save ourselves, in judging others, and by insisting that we must be in control. Lent is a time for remembering—remembering that we are mortal.

My husband Roger and I were all set to be perfect pilgrims. But, alas, we had plenty of opportunities to be humbled and reminded of our mortality all along the *Camino*. We had sore feet. We were hungry. We were thirsty. There were days when we collapsed on our beds thinking we could not take another step. But somehow we would rise the next morning, pack up, and hit the road.

The Desert Fathers were early Christian monks, hermits who lived austere lives of prayer and devotion in the desert. There is a story about one of them who was asked what the monks did all day. He replied, "We fall down and get up; we fall down and get up; we fall down and get up."

As we begin our Lenten journey, perhaps what we need most to do is to remember that we are only human. We will fall and get up again—multiple times.

The Week of Ash Wednesday

Lent, just like life itself, is not a direct ascent to a mountaintop experience of Easter but is a winding pilgrimage with God to a deeper humanity, helping us fully live into who and how God has created us to be.

We all have our vulnerabilities. We all make mistakes. Like Roger and I on the first day of the *Camino*, we all get lost. Most of us will fail to meet our personal expectations for a "Holy Lent." But that's okay. A human Lent is a holy Lent. We don't need to save ourselves. We can let go of that. That is God's job, not ours. We just need to put one foot in front of the other, take life one step, one minute, one day at a time and do the best we can, trusting that God will provide for our needs. We are simply human. God doesn't want us to be anything more than that—or anything less. God loves us exactly as we are.

Almighty and everlasting God, you hate nothing you have made and forgive the sins of all who are penitent: Create and make in us new and contrite hearts, that we, worthily lamenting our sins and acknowledging our wretchedness, may obtain of you, the God of all mercy, perfect remission and forgiveness; through Jesus Christ our Lord, who lives and reigns with you and the Holy Spirit, one God, for ever and ever. **Amen.**

The Book of Common Prayer

Are We There Yet?

Pilgrim's Journal
Suggested practices for the week

Make a list of all the ways you "play God" in your life. Ask God to take back these things that rightly belong to God, not you.

Recite Psalm 103 or another psalm while walking, rocking in a chair, or doing some other repetitive task. Notice how the words take on the rhythm of your body.

Write a love letter to yourself. Acknowledge your faults, your shortcomings, your simple humanity, and the fact that you are loved—in other words, look at yourself as God sees you.

Make a list of things you need to let go of. Ask God to guide you to both tangible and intangible things—a memory that hurts, the lure of a clean house, the clutter of old clothes. At the end of the week, delete or rip up the list. Let them go.

Look at your calendar for the season of Lent as if it were a guidebook. Do you know where you are going? What is the goal of this Lenten pilgrimage? Do your chosen Lenten disciplines support the goal? Do adjustments need to be made to those disciplines—or to your life?

Day 2

There is a scene in the movie *Wild* when Cheryl Strayed, played by Reese Witherspoon, is in a motel room with her gear strewn across two beds as she prepares for her hike on the Pacific Crest Trail. She zips the final compartment of her pack, tightens the straps, and lifts it—or, more accurately, tries to lift it. The pack won't budge. This is not an uncommon experience for travelers. Many of us overpack, taking more than we could ever actually need. Testifying to this truth, lodgings along the *Camino* contain closets or piles of items that pilgrims have discarded along their journey.

On the *Camino*, we learned how little we truly need. We took only a few shirts, a couple pairs of pants, three pairs of socks, rain gear, and some toiletries. An iPhone served as camera, computer, phone, and travel journal. That was about the long and short of our packing list. We traveled lightly, but we wanted for nothing.

We follow Jesus into the wilderness every Lent, hoping to home in on what we truly need in this life. It is so easy to find ourselves overburdened, not only with the tangible stuff of life but also with the emotional weight we carry—guilt, resentments, worries, over-functioning tendencies, the unarticulated or imagined expectations of others, and false images of ourselves. The backpacks of our lives grow much too heavy. Lent is a time for unpacking our burdens—a time for letting them go.

In medieval times, some pilgrims walked the *Camino* as an act of penance, in order to be freed from grievous, mortal sins; others walked, praying for a miracle, and many died along the way. Modern-day pilgrims have all sorts of reasons for walking—adventure, celebrations of retirement, mourning losses. My husband and I walked to mark the transition of our home to an empty nest. We were finding a gentle way to let go of our years of active parenting, grieving and celebrating at the same time. And we were renewing our own partnership for the new journey ahead. By traveling lightly, we freed ourselves to more closely follow Jesus.

God, lighten our loads. Give us grace this Lent to let go of those things we carry that do not serve us or serve you, and to hold onto what is good and true. Help us to remember Jesus' words: "Come to me all you who are weary and are carrying heavy burdens, and I will give you rest...my yoke is easy, and my burden is light." **Amen**.

Day 3

One of the first things we needed to let go of was our tendency to judge others. We carried backpacks, but there were some pilgrims who had their packs taxied from town to town. Others walked the *Camino* with tour groups, and their suitcases were transported from one luxury hotel to another. Others rode bikes. Many walked only the final hundred kilometers of the *Camino*, the minimum distance required to obtain a *Compostela* certificate. It was tempting to judge these folks, as if we were somehow stronger or holier. In the case of those tour groups, maybe we just envied them their change of clothes in the evenings!

It's so easy—and so human—to judge others in order to make ourselves feel better and inflate our self-worth. Equally insidious are the ways we compare ourselves to others and find ourselves deficient. We rarely stayed in *albergues*, the traditional *Camino* pilgrim lodgings. Instead we found inexpensive hotels where we could have a private room, thereby avoiding the snoring of strangers, crowds, and shared bathrooms. I sometimes asked myself if we were taking it too easy, not having the "real" *Camino* experience. This was the wrong way to look at our choice.

The *Camino* transcends many of the normal divisions of everyday life. Pilgrims come from all nationalities, religious faiths, and ages. Some travel alone, others walk in groups. Some are constantly socializing, and others want to be left alone. All of these sorts and conditions of pilgrims are accepted and respected. A bond developed between us and our fellow pilgrims, even those with whom we could barely communicate—the Happy Korean, the Kissing Italians, and the two German pilgrims the age of our own children with whom we walked for several days. We didn't know their socioeconomic background or political leanings. We were simply fellow pilgrims.

There is a saying, "Everyone has their own *Camino*." This is a good lesson for our Lenten journey and for all of life. Each person is unique—uniquely called and loved by God. We need to let go—to be purged—of the ways we compare and judge others, and ourselves, too. Judgment is God's job, not ours.

O God, you made us in your own image and redeemed us through Jesus your Son: Look with compassion on the whole human family; take away the arrogance and hatred which infect our hearts; break down the walls that separate us; unite us in bonds of love; and work through our struggle and confusion to accomplish your purposes on earth; that, in your good time, all nations and races may serve you in harmony around your heavenly throne; through Jesus Christ our Lord. **Amen.**

The Book of Common Prayer

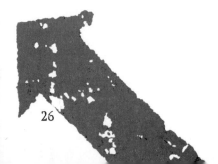

Are We There Yet?

Day 4

I cannot help but wonder about ancient pilgrims from all over Europe who were ordered by their parish priests to walk the *Camino* as penance. I wonder what sins they committed. Burglary? Adultery? Murder? What sin could be bad enough to risk life and limb, to leave families and farms in search of forgiveness? Many of those pilgrims never arrived back home.

The irony is that we walked the *Camino* for fun and adventure. We spent hard-earned money, used vacation and sabbatical time, and looked forward to the trip with great anticipation. True, we had sore muscles and aching feet at the end of each day, but we defined true hardship as a bumpy mattress or four hours without a stop for a *café con leche*!

Our experiences were removed by hundreds of years and radically different cultural circumstances, but it's still a good reminder—one person's penance can be another person's pleasure. In the same way that everyone has his or her own *Camino*, each one of us needs to sort out, in partnership with God, what our own spiritual practices for our Lenten observance will look and feel like.

I remember a parishioner who was deciding how she would observe Lent. What should she give up—should she fast, or maybe start volunteering at the soup kitchen? Her husband had died weeks before her visit to me, and she had spent the previous year as a caregiver. I told her that it sounded like Lent for her might best be observed by giving herself a break—to rest and allow God to love her.

The destination of our Lenten pilgrimage is not a cathedral but the holy place of Easter joy. How each of us arrives at this holy spot will depend on our personalities, our stage in life, and our circumstances. Some people need rigorous discipline to order their lives, and others need to let go of rigidity and rigor to experience life more fully. We all need to repent—to examine ourselves, to study scripture, and to pray. But exactly what form these spiritual practices take for each of us requires careful discernment and prayerful listening.

Lord Jesus Christ, you call each one of us by name.
You know our needs and know us better than we know
ourselves. Guide each of us in our Lenten pilgrimage, that
we might listen for your voice and faithfully follow where
you lead. Lead us to that place of freedom and Easter joy.
Amen.

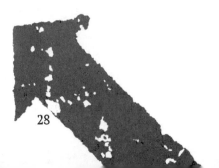

Are We There Yet?

The First Week in Lent
Forgiveness and Freedom

Then the LORD God said, "See, the man has become like one of us, knowing good and evil; and now, he might reach out his hand and take also from the tree of life, and eat, and live forever"—therefore the LORD God sent him forth from the garden of Eden, to till the ground from which he was taken. He drove out the man; and at the east of the garden of Eden he placed the cherubim, and a sword flaming and turning to guard the way to the tree of life.

Genesis 3:22-24

The Journey

This photograph represents my work leading pilgrimages to historic lynching sites in the American South. This particular photo features me (on the left), Bishop Rob Wright of the Episcopal Diocese of Atlanta, and one of the pilgrims. On this day, we were visiting the Jonathan Daniels Remembrance Site in Hayneville, Alabama. Our pilgrimage through these sites is about bearing witness to these places, speaking the names of the martyrs who died there, and praying for the perpetrators of these crimes. Our hope is that we can learn from and with each other about racism, violence, and how we can live more fully into the beloved community to which Jesus calls us. These are holy acts of reconciliation and peacemaking.

Catherine Meeks

Day 5

As an Arkansas sharecropper's daughter who rose before the sun in order to watch it come up over the nearby trees, I had no idea what it meant to be a pilgrim. But I was destined to be one.

This inner sense of seeing myself in a world I needed to understand forced me out of bed to pray and seek the beauty of stillness. I needed to see the sunrise and the world waking up, the small birds and other animals emerging for their own daily pilgrimages in search of food and whatever they needed to make their way through the day.

My little girl self was not sure who God was, but I knew there was something bigger than me out in the world, and I wanted to reach out to that force. I lived on a white man's land with my mother and father who were trying to create the best life possible for us. My parents urged us to seek the goodness of God in spite of hardships and setbacks. They were vigilant pilgrims, although I seriously doubt either of them would have called themselves that.

The heart seeks and trusts that it will find companions along the way. The seeking of my own heart led me forward and into the next steps of the journey, though for many years I had no language to describe the thirst propelling me along the path.

It would take me years to come to a place where I could reflect upon the wonder of that young country girl rising in the morning before daybreak, just to pray and watch the world wake up.

Come, let us sing to the LORD; let us shout for joy to the Rock of our salvation. Let us come before his presence with thanksgiving and raise a loud shout to him with psalms.

For the LORD is a great God, and a great King above all gods. In his hand are the caverns of the earth, and the heights of the hills are his also. The sea is his, for he made it, and his hands have molded the dry land.

Come, let us bow down, and bend the knee, and kneel before the LORD our Maker. For he is our God, and we are the people of his pasture and the sheep of his hand. Oh, that today you would hearken to his voice!

Psalm 95:1-7

Are We There Yet?

Pilgrim's Journal
Suggested practices for the week

Return home from church, work, or running errands via new routes. Visit different grocery stores, department stores, or restaurants.

Sit in a quiet place and reflect on your journey—see if any forgotten memories rise to the surface and jot them down.

Reflect upon the idea of being a pilgrim in your heart and the relationship between a heart-journey and a physical pilgrimage.

Holy God, may my heart stay open to the idea of being on a journey through this life and may there be grace and courage to sustain that journey each day. May I focus my energy and attention on the journey more than arriving at a destination. **Amen.**

Day 6

No pilgrimage is possible without an awakened heart. The heart knows that life on this planet is a journey inward and outward. An awakened heart knows there will be more questions than answers—we have to learn to embrace the questions with loving-kindness in order to find the pathway to the answers.

These answers are for the deep questions that begin in the hearts of youngsters: Why is the sky blue? Where does the wind go when we don't feel it? Why do bad things happen to good people? How can bad people have good luck? Why is life unfair? The list grows longer as our journey deepens. There are times when we may feel that all of life can be summed up with one big question mark.

But in the midst of the questioning—and the pain that can arise from having more questions than answers—comes a burst of awareness. From our deepest selves, we attain a deep inner realization that life is a journey, and every thing on this planet is on a pilgrimage. All of life is moving from birth to

Are We There Yet?

death. Of course, cycles and rhythms keep everything from dying at the same time. But the cycle of birth, death, and rebirth is inevitable. The awakened heart knows that life on this planet is a journey. Awakened, the heart embarks upon the path with joy and expectation.

Holy God, as my awakened heart turns toward you, I seek to learn to be patient toward what is unsolved in my heart, to live into your answers, and to make my heart able to hear them. **Amen.**

Day 7

✳

My father's broken heart informed his entire life. Living in such close proximity to this man, whom I both loved and feared, his brokenheartedness spurred me on a journey to find greater wellness than I experienced in my relationship to Daddy.

My father's heart was broken when my twelve-year-old brother died from the lack of prompt and adequate medical care to deal with appendicitis. Proper care was unavailable for my brother because he was a poor black child in rural Arkansas. When my brother was taken to the local hospital in the town eighteen miles away from our home, he was turned away. The doctors instead insisted we take my brother to the charity hospital in another town, seventy miles away. We didn't have a car and by the time my father arranged to have my brother transported, it was too late. My brother had died.

For any parent, the sense of brokenness and immobilization brought on by the loss of a child—and a loss that could have been prevented—would be almost insurmountable.

My father's grief over the death of his son proved especially difficult for him—a poor, illiterate sharecropper. But I learned valuable lessons from this tragedy that have sustained my lifetime pilgrimage of seeking wellness.

In this season of reflection, we are presented a perfect time to think about the role of brokenheartedness in our lives. Where have the broken places led to opportunities for healing? How have those broken places helped and hindered as we faced limitations—our own and those imposed by others? Can new life grow in the cracks created by brokenness?

Holy God, though brokenness can lead to new strength, save me from trials that are immobilizing. May the trials that come be accompanied by enough grace to create the energy that I need to stand with courage and steadfastness. **Amen.**

Day 8

As pilgrims traveling through this barren land, it is critical to name the ones upon whose shoulders we stand in order to stay faithful to the path unfolding before us. We make an unfortunate mistake in assuming we can make the journey on our own. No matter what form the development of community takes for each pilgrim, there is a constant necessity to affirm and acknowledge those who have walked and paved the path before us.

In America, an entire group of folks has gone on before us but are seldom acknowledged because of the terror and violence that was visited upon them. These are the men and women—some white, but mostly black—who were the victims of the various acts of terror that came to be characterized as lynchings.

While the lynched person on rare occasions had committed a crime, people were lynched for standing up for the rights of others, for being in the wrong place, or just for being black.

Pilgrimages to historical lynching sites in memory of the many victims are needed. Those who were lost must be remembered and have their names called out aloud. Regardless of the particular facts of each situation, these men and women are martyrs whose persecution is rarely acknowledged. They cannot rest until we remember them—and neither can we.

Modern-day pilgrims who are attempting to dismantle oppression in sustainable ways must pay attention to the meaning of this cloud of witnesses and the ways in which they lost their lives. And along our journey to remembering them, we must make sure that such atrocities never happen again.

Holy God, grant this day that I will have eyes to see and ears to hear of the great cloud of witnesses that surround me as I travel this path. Help me to remember the ones who suffered beyond words and to hold their memory in my heart. May we all find healing as we remember. **Amen.**

Day 9

While the lynching pilgrimages I have organized help us to remember this terrible and tragic history, these pilgrimages also call us to move into new frontiers, both individually and collectively. Frontiers are those borderlands between places, understandings, hearts, and minds, where imagination and innovation meet intention, in places like Galilee or Damascus. Pilgrims from England and Holland sailed across the Atlantic Ocean and climbed the Appalachian Mountains to cross new frontiers in faith, just as today's pilgrims from Mexico and Syria cross rivers and seas to pursue their lives of faith in places as diverse as Dallas or Dayton.

Pilgrims have to stay alert to apathy and inertia. It is all too easy to stay in the comfortable place—emotionally, physically, and spiritually—of privilege. The mere act of showing up for the sojourn can be an opportunity to break open places of internal stagnation. This kind of breaking and brokenness makes it possible for new frontiers to be imagined and embraced.

The value of paying attention to every invitation to embrace a new frontier is verified by heaven itself. When we accept an invitation to see and live into a new frontier, our lives change—and then will change again. We see this truth written across the face of the seasons, the limbs of trees, in flowers, and all the way down to the amount of hair in a dog's coat and number of feathers on a bird. Though some of the changes are easier than others to accept, they all demand movement. The place of comfort and ease must shift.

An enthusiastic "yes" to the beckoning call of a new frontier requires courage. But that courageous response is the first step toward a life with the capacity to be lived in peace.

Holy God, as I stand in the security of the firm foundation that you have provided for me as your child, give me the courage to say yes to the call of the frontier, which will lead me on the pilgrim's path toward all that you have prepared for me. I seek your gift of courage. **Amen.**

Day 10

We have great freedom to jump in our cars, catch a train, bus, or airplane and travel to wherever we wish. But some of the greatest distances that are to be traveled lie between the head and the heart. The capacity to allow this journey to develop in the soul is formative in creating ways we can stand in the world and navigate our lives. This kind of inner pilgrimage requires courage, faith, and a deep sense of self.

Many will experience moments of doubt—even the bravest pilgrims among us—but doubt must never have the final word. The journey begins with a willingness to listen to the still, small, inner voices of our hearts, to pay attention to our dreams, to explore the root causes of conflicts in our homes and communities, and to search for the sound of our own genuine voices. This journey, though difficult, can also bring great reward and deliver to us the treasure of a deep and abiding sense of peace.

This peace, God's own good peace, defies understanding because it is often found in the midst of circumstances that should cause great distress. But instead, we experience stillness and calm, as an unexpected spirit arises from the depths of our hearts—a gift from the heavens.

Holy God, let me not hide myself from the richness of this journey by being unwilling to go on the long inner journey with you. As I travel in my physical body from place to place, let me courageously travel in my mind and spirit. May I have the same faith, confidence, and commitment for this inner journey that I have for the external journeys that I travel to by car, train, plane, or foot. **Amen.**

Day 11

The internal and external journeys of the pilgrim can bring pain. Many times, it will be difficult for us to believe that joy will come in the morning. But there is joy too in the persistent and dogged determination to stay on the pilgrim path, a journey of too many questions and too few answers, of lost relationships and ideas, and long periods of moving from frontier to frontier without a clear picture about where home might be found.

I have made a long journey to joy. Much like the author and theologian C.S. Lewis declared in the title of his marvelous book, *Surprised by Joy: The Shape of My Early Life*, I have also been surprised by joy. Oddly enough, the joy has arisen from finally arriving at a place of acceptance.

I have accepted the the fluidity of life, the necessity for the frontier, and the willingness to rest in the unsolved heart puzzles. Though I lament our brokenness in how we deal with matters of race, class, and gender; the long, dark pilgrimage toward dismantling oppression has led to new light in my life.

Are We There Yet?

Though the new light has not fixed everything, its bright and liberating rays make it possible for me to see the path a bit more clearly and invigorates the way in which I walk upon it.

The new light brought the morning—and there is joy.

Holy God, the pain of the journey can be daunting. Thank you for the light that comes. Thank you for the gift of sustaining hope that each new day, with its questions, challenges, pain, and sorrows, belongs to you—just as I belong to you. Thank you for the possibility of this joy and for all the glimpses of it. **Amen.**

The Second Week in Lent
Devotion and Discovery

After a long time the king of Egypt died. The Israelites groaned under their slavery, and cried out. Out of the slavery their cry for help rose up to God. God heard their groaning, and God remembered his covenant with Abraham, Isaac, and Jacob. God looked upon the Israelites, and God took notice of them.

Exodus 2:23-25

The Journey

I never imagined that a promise to the Blessed Virgin Mary would lead me on pilgrimages across two continents to shrines built for the glory of God and in memory of her life and ministry. Over the years, a devotion to Our Lord's Mother has been a key component in my spiritual growth and development as a disciple of Jesus Christ. This has led me on pilgrimages to two shrines dedicated to Our Lady of Walsingham, one in England and the other in the United States. The stories of both shrines reveal a fascinating history of faith and trust, of healing and of love. A benefit of the modern age of the Internet is that both shrines have well-maintained websites with additional information and pictures. I encourage you to explore the sites and consider a pilgrimage to one of them. You can read more about them by visiting www.walsinghamanglican.org.uk or www.gracesheboygan.com.

Jeffrey Queen

Day 12

I still remember the groaning, but it didn't begin that way.

The whole trouble started a couple of days earlier, with a red patch of skin about the size of a dollar coin on my bicep. Now, my whole right arm was hot, angry, about twice its size, and filled with infection. I was lying on my back on one of those moveable tabletops connected to the hospital's MRI machine.

I was half aware, the fever having a strong grip on my body as well as my mind, but I knew the diagnosis couldn't be good. Chief surgeons aren't supposed to be in radiology labs this late at night. I heard strange voices talking about amputation, about cutting until they found clean tissue with no infection.

They can't be talking about me, I thought. *I'm a priest. I can't lose my arm. How can I give the blessing at the end of the Eucharist without my right arm?*

Then silence.

I was back in the intensive care unit. *Is that my wife standing next to me? Who is that with her? It's the deacon from church. Are they reading Compline?*

"We have sinned against you, through our own fault, in thought, and word, and deed." Weakly, I join in saying the prayers. I've never known it so difficult to think or speak.

What is going on with me? I don't have the energy to continue speaking the prayer. I'm too tired. I am afraid. I've never felt like this. Did I just groan? I must have. My wife is holding my hand and looking down at me.

Darkness.

How long have I been asleep? Is that a bell ringing?

In my mind, the words form. They are not as muddled by the fever and the pain:

The Angel of the Lord brought tidings to Mary. And she conceived by the Holy Spirit.

I might be too weak to pray out loud, but I know the Angelus, and I can still pray it in my thoughts. *Hail Mary, full of grace, the Lord is with thee. Blessed art thou amongst women and blessed is the fruit of thy womb, Jesus. Holy Mary, Mother of God, pray for us sinners now and at the hour of our death. Amen.*

The Israelites know something about crying out to God. They groan under each pharaoh until God sends Moses to deliver them and lead them on a great pilgrimage out of Egypt and into the Promised Land.

Are We There Yet?

Mary knows what it means to cry out to God in despair. She groans as her son dies on the tree. She holds his lifeless body in her arms after he has been beaten and tortured. Her pilgrimage is one of a mother's love, her hopes and dreams poured out for her child.

Even Jesus knows what it means to cry out. He groans with the weight of the world's sins, which we seem eager to pile on him day after day. His pilgrimage is one of incarnation, of movement through his life—and of gathering a community who will face rejection for following him and suffer for proclaiming his good news. Yet the pilgrim road Jesus walks— and that we walk as his disciples—always leads to resurrection.

The motif of life as pilgrimage is firmly rooted in the lives of the saints and can easily be seen in the life of Jesus and his movement through the Judean countryside and his ultimate destination—Jerusalem. Jesus bids all his followers to take this journey with him; he sets his face toward Jerusalem and extends his life to us with the gentle words: *Come and see.*

But are we brave enough to journey with him?

One thing about pilgrimage I am most grateful for is that it is rarely, if ever, done alone. That night in the hospital, I was not alone. My wife was with me—holding my hand in comfort, determined to find a way through suffering into healing and wholeness. The deacon was there, carrying the prayers of the entire parish, joining them with her own. Jesus was there with me that night, just as he is when anyone suffers, bringing healing and hope. Mary was there with me, too. As I prayed the Angelus in the ICU, I saw Mary standing before me. I promised her that if I recovered, I would seek her out and give thanks for her assistance in Jesus' healing of my body.

The next morning, the doctors were more optimistic than they had been the night before. The antibiotics finally seemed to be working. It looked as if I would not lose my arm to the infection, after all. Another day, and the infection started to recede. My fever broke on the fourth day. All in all, I was in the hospital for twelve days (four in intensive care). I went home and spent another fourteen days on intravenous antibiotics.

The doctors never discovered what caused the infection; they had started me on an antibiotic cocktail before they could even culture it. But I knew Jesus had healed me, and I had his mother to thank.

At the end of the Angelus is the prayer for Annunciation. In this prayer, we see the familiar pilgrim pattern—the movement that begins with the life of Jesus and takes us through his death, passion, and resurrection. The prayer assumes that we are making this pilgrimage with Jesus. Honestly, I can't think of a better pattern for a life of faith than one spent in pilgrimage.

We are on a journey, with Jesus and the saints as our guides. The pilgrim road, like the journey of Lent, leads to resurrection and the measureless depth of Easter joy.

Pilgrim's Journal
Suggested practice for the week

Incorporate the Angelus into your daily prayers.

V. The Angel of the Lord brought tidings to Mary.
R. And she conceived of the Holy Spirit.
Hail Mary, full of grace, the Lord is with thee.
Blessed art thou amongst women,
and blessed is the fruit of thy womb, Jesus.
Holy Mary, Mother of God, pray for us sinners,
now and at the hour of our death. Amen.

V. Behold the handmaid of the Lord.
R. Be it unto me according to thy word.
Hail Mary, full of grace, the Lord is with thee…

V. And the Word was made Flesh.
R. And dwelt among us.
Hail Mary, full of grace, the Lord is with thee…

V. Pray for us, O holy Mother of God.
R. *That we may be made worthy of the promises of Christ.*

We beseech Thee O Lord, pour thy grace into our hearts, that as we have known the Incarnation of thy Son our Lord Jesus Christ by the message of an angel, so by his +Cross and passion we may be brought to the glory of his Resurrection; through the same Christ Our Lord. **Amen.**

Pour your grace into our hearts, O Lord, that we who have known the incarnation of your Son Jesus Christ, announced by an angel to the Virgin Mary, may by his cross and passion be brought to the glory of his resurrection; who lives and reigns with you, in the unity of the Holy Spirit, one God, now and for ever. **Amen.**

The Book of Common Prayer

Are We There Yet?

Day 13

Have you ever tried to sing a hymn with thirty-seven verses while standing still? Honestly, doing so is not the most enjoyable activity. Don't misunderstand me: I love to sing and I really love to sing hymns, but thirty-seven verses can make even the most die-hard hymn lover antsy. So began my introduction to the devotion of the Ever Blessed Virgin Mary, Our Lady of Walsingham.

Rain fell heavily throughout the Saturday morning of my first visit to one of the most famous American Marian shrines—Our Lady of Walsingham. Because of the weather, we could not "take the Lady out for a stroll," as was the custom of the annual pilgrimage held the second weekend of October each year at Grace Episcopal Church in Sheboygan, Wisconsin.

The stroll is part of the service of Holy Eucharist, which begins with a procession led by four students from the Episcopal seminary of Nashotah House. The students carry the carved image of Mary through the streets of Sheboygan. On this year, Mary stood in the crossing of the parish church, protected from the deluge outside.

In my opinion, she looked a little frustrated, but maybe I was projecting my disappointment onto her. This was my first time—and being a good tourist, I wanted the full show! The problem with this attitude is that I wasn't attending the pilgrimage as a tourist.

A tourist would naturally want to take something as a keepsake. I was a pilgrim and had promised to give something back to Jesus and Our Lady in gratitude for my healing. Had I already lost my way?

The Walsingham Pilgrim's Hymn tells the history of the Marian Shrine in Little Walsingham in Norfolk, England, after which the American shrine is modeled. One of the verses makes reference to Henry VIII, who would eventually destroy the English shrine.

> *But at last came a King who had greed in his eyes*
> *And he lusted for treasure with fraud and with lies.*

I realized in that moment that I too had come to take something from Our Lady rather than give something back. What I needed to give back was a sacrifice of praise and thanksgiving for the miracle of healing in my life.

Why are we always more ready to receive than to give? Why are we always more ready to hoard than to share?

Where is God calling us to give? How are we willing or unwilling to answer that call?

Jesus' pilgrimage to resurrection first leads to the cross, the greatest gift of all. If we want to walk alongside him, we also must be ready to give.

Let your Spirit, O Lord, come into the midst of us to wash us with the pure water of repentance, and prepare us to be always a living sacrifice to you; through Jesus Christ our Lord, who lives and reigns with you and the Holy Spirit, one God, for ever and ever. **Amen.**

Lesser Feasts and Fasts

Day 14

One of the regular components of the Walsingham Pilgrimage as celebrated at the Sheboygan site is the Friday Quiet Day. Typically the preacher for the weekend offers meditations at noon and 3 p.m. At six p.m., a Solemn Evensong with Benediction is offered by the parish choir, which is joined by the student choir from the seminary at Nashotah House.

During one of these meditations, our preacher said it was necessary for us "to bring Mary out of the shed." His assertion was that Mary is only brought out once a year with the nativity sets and Christmas decorations, and after Advent and Christmas are over, she is promptly returned to the shed. I was struck by this example—both by its truth and its imagery.

How often am I guilty of packing up the very things that bring wholeness in my life? How quickly do I stow them out of sight because I'm not ready to fully embrace the life they are calling me to lead?

Are We There Yet?

If the internal and external movement of pilgrimage is a fitting motif for the Christian life, then obstinacy and intransigence might be fitting antitheses.

Too often, I like the obstacles that keep me off the pilgrim road. I'm unwilling to change old habits and behaviors because I believe the pain of movement to be greater than the bedsores of complacency. But Mary calls out to me from the same shed where I store much of what challenges my complacency. She instructs me as she did the servants at the wedding at Cana in Galilee, "Do whatever Jesus tells you."

Am I ready to accept the call? Have I grown too comfortable, too friendly with the obstacles along the way? Can I readily say yes, just as Mary did when she replies to God's call to the pilgrim road with her memorable words, "Behold, the handmaid of the Lord. Be it unto me according to your word?"

O God, you willed to redeem us from all iniquity by your Son: Deliver us when we are tempted to regard sin without abhorrence, and let the virtue of his passion come between us and our mortal enemy; through Jesus Christ our Lord, who lives and reigns with you and the Holy Spirit, one God, for ever and ever. **Amen.**

Lesser Feasts and Fasts

Day 15

✳

In 1061, the Blessed Virgin Mary appeared to a Saxon noblewoman in the English countryside. In the vision, the Blessed Mother asked this woman—Richeldis de Faverches—to build a house. It was to be modeled upon the structure in which Mary received the Annunciation from the angel Gabriel that she would give birth to the Son of God.

After some struggle and a miracle of sorts in the means of construction, the Holy House (as it would become known) was completed. Almost immediately, this humble structure became a place of pilgrimage. A water well with curative properties was discovered on the site of the Holy House. People brought the sick and infirm for healing. As travel to Jerusalem proved more and more difficult, "England's Nazareth" quickly became a place of prayer for all, and devotion to Our Lady of Walsingham was born.

Healing continues to be a central charism of both the English and American shrines. Both communities have a lively and active prayer ministry. And at each location, healing prayers

Are We There Yet?

are offered as requests come in from around the globe. These intercessions are offered in the context of daily prayers said in the shrines. As is the case when heaven and earth are brought near to one another, stories of answered prayers abound.

Healing is what first brought me to Our Lady of Walsingham. I can't explain or rationalize it—all I know is that my body was shutting down because of a life-threatening staph infection, and then suddenly it wasn't. I made a promise to seek a shrine to the Blessed Virgin Mary and to offer thanks for my healing. I also wanted to make a public witness to a moment in my life when heaven and earth came near to one another.

On the drive home from that first trip to the American proto-shrine in Wisconsin, I came to understand that where love, prayer, and faith are lived out in community, the gap between heaven and earth becomes very narrow. I also realized that the pilgrim road is not just about going on a faraway journey—it is also about returning home transformed. I began asking myself, "What can I do to foster a community of prayer in the place I call home? How can the place I worship God become a place of healing and wholeness?" My pilgrim journey helps me to see what healing can be about.

In *Death Comes for the Archbishop*, author Willa Cather offers this up for our consideration: "The Miracles of the Church seem to me to rest not so much upon faces or voices or healing power coming suddenly near to us from afar off, but upon our perceptions being made finer, so that for a moment our eyes can see and our ears can hear what is there about us always."

O God, you so loved the world that you gave your only-begotten Son to reconcile earth with heaven: Grant that we, loving you above all things, may love our friends in you, and our enemies for your sake; through Jesus Christ our Lord, who lives and reigns with you and the Holy Spirit, one God, for ever and ever. **Amen.**

Lesser Feasts and Fasts

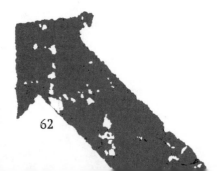

Are We There Yet?

Day 16

Pilgrimages force us to engage all five senses—sight, sound, smell, taste, and touch.

These journeys are meant to be overwhelming—they are meant to lead us into action.

The Shrine Church in Walsingham, England, was illumined on a chilly February evening. The Angelus bell broke the silence; the smell of incense and beeswax candles recalled centuries of worship to God. I tasted the bread and wine during the opening eucharist and touched the worn stone pavers trod by so many pilgrims before me. This great feast of the senses made for a fully immersive experience as I made my first journey to this small English village.

The Shrine of Our Lady of Walsingham is tucked away in a remote part of the Norfolk countryside near a place locally known as The Wash. My first visit took place during a priests' and deacons' retreat held each year during a week leading up to Lent. Each day of the retreat includes quiet time, a meditation on the theme for the week, conversations during lunch and dinner, and somewhere between four and five hours of worship and prayer to God in the Shrine Church. This focused activity lends itself to creating a holy space where spiritual experience and physical exertion are joined into one seamless, unnamable grace.

As Christians in the Western tradition, our spiritual lives often become merely intellectual exercises. This unfortunately means our lives of faith can occur wholly within our thoughts and intentions, never being made manifest in our living flesh and blood.

How often am I guilty of having read the Daily Office out of *The Book of Common Prayer* without uttering a sound? When have I been stirred by a godly, spirit-filled sermon, only to do nothing about applying it to my daily life? When have I stood by when a hurting and broken world called out for help?

Bishop Frank Weston, famed Anglo-Catholic leader of the early twentieth century, says it this way:

> Jesus on the Throne of his glory, Jesus in the Blessed Sacrament, Jesus received into your hearts in Communion, Jesus with you mystically as you pray, and Jesus enthroned in the hearts and bodies of his brothers and sisters up and down this country. And it is folly—it is madness—to suppose that you can worship Jesus in the Sacraments and Jesus on the Throne of glory, when you are sweating him in the souls and bodies of his children. It cannot be done.

Are We There Yet?

There then, as I conceive it, is your present duty; and I beg you, brethren, as you love the Lord Jesus…Go out and look for Jesus in the ragged, in the naked, in the oppressed and sweated, in those who have lost hope, in those who are struggling to make good. Look for Jesus. And when you see him, gird yourselves with his towel and try to wash their feet.

The pilgrim road leads each of us on a journey. This road leads from the place where our thoughts and intentions originate into love made active and real in the places where we live and in the people that we cherish.

O Lord, strong and mighty, Lord of hosts and King of glory: Cleanse our hearts from sin, keep our hands pure, and turn our minds from what is passing away; so that at the last we may stand in your holy place and receive your blessing; through Jesus Christ our Lord, who lives and reigns with you and the Holy Spirit, one God, for ever and ever. **Amen.**

Lesser Feasts and Fasts

Day 17

A deeply moving aspect of any visit to the Shrine Church at Walsingham is the noon Holy Hour, featuring prayers before the reserved sacrament.

This time begins in silence. After the Angelus is said, a passage of scripture is offered as a way to focus meditation and devotion. Then for the next hour, pilgrims spend time in silent prayer.

During this time, some offer their prayers kneeling; others kneel for a time before returning to a seat. Occasionally, a weary pilgrim will offer a prayer in the form of a snore. The emphasis in this devotional exercise is simply being with Jesus.

In a world that is at work twenty-four hours a day and a church that increasingly finds its identity in the amount of mission and ministry performed, Holy Hour can be a hard sell. Spending an hour in seeming inactivity can be problematic. And yet, we would never consider trying to grow a plant without time each day in sunlight. Why then would we consider living a full Christian life without regular time in the presence of the Son?

I was excited to host a recent visit from our bishop. It was his first experience in the parish where I serve. The congregation is very active, both inside and outside the walls of the church. After a fantastic visitation, I sat down for lunch with the bishop, awaiting the praise I knew he would give the congregation.

"What do you think about the parish?" I asked.

"They look tired, " he replied.

This was not the response I was expecting. Even so, I could not help but realize he was right. We *were* all busy—with work, school, play, living, partnering together in our various levels of success. Maybe what we needed was a little rest, some quiet time.

The bishop's visitation took place on the first Sunday in Lent. On the evening of Maundy Thursday, the parish joined in a prayer vigil extending into the hours of Good Friday—a modified Holy Hour, with parishioners committing to a time of prayer before the Sacrament.

At a simple Altar of Repose, pilgrims came and went, spending some quiet time with Jesus, in commemoration of his time in Gethsemane. It was the first time this devotion took place in our congregation. By the overwhelming response, it won't be the last.

The pilgrim road leads to many places. Sometimes it leads the pilgrim weary from movement to a hostel, or a hearth, or to the heart of Jesus, giving the one who sojourns a moment of refreshment in the presence of the Son of God. Take a moment of rest today to find yourself in the open arms of Jesus.

Grant, O Lord, that as your Son Jesus Christ prayed for his enemies on the cross, so we may have grace to forgive those who wrongfully or scornfully use us, that we ourselves may be able to receive your forgiveness; through Jesus Christ our Lord, who lives and reigns with you and the Holy Spirit, one God, for ever and ever. **Amen.**

Lesser Feasts and Fasts

Are We There Yet?

Day 18

In his prologue to *The Canterbury Tales*, Geoffrey Chaucer says that with the coming of spring, so comes the urge for pilgrimage:

> *When the sweet showers of April have pierced*
> *the drought of March and pierced it to the root.*
>
> *And when the west wind too with its sweet breath*
> *has given life in every wood and field.*
>
> *Then people long to go on pilgrimages,*
> *and palmers to take ship for foreign shores,*
> *and distant shrines, famous in different lands;*
> *And most especially, from all the shires*
> *Of England, to Canterbury they come,*
> *The holy blessed martyr there to seek.*
>
> *To Canterbury, and pay devout homage,*
> *there came at nightfall to the hostelry*
> *some nine-and-twenty in a company,*
> *Folk of all kinds, met in accidental*
> *companionship, for they were pilgrims all.*

The pilgrim road leads to many destinations—places of healing, forgiveness, service and also to rest and refreshment. Winding and wending, it can also lead to companionship and friendship.

Various pilgrim roads often have a badge or other token to identify the pilgrims making their journey. They can be as complex as the scallop shell and credential of the *Camino* or as simple as the palm branch carried by those setting off for Jerusalem—as noted by Chaucer's reference to "palmers."

For me, one of the most identifying marks of the pilgrim is friendship. In my journeys to Sheboygan and Walsingham and beyond, my greatest accomplishments are the friendships I have made along the way. Our shared stories and experiences have added such deep layers to my own pilgrim road. And when I have wandered off the path, a fellow pilgrim has offered a helping hand to bring me back onto the Way.

We should sit up and take notice that Jesus calls us friends and not servants. We are not only called into friendship with Christ Jesus—we are also called into friendship with fellow pilgrims we meet along the way. Sometimes our friends are the pillars who support us in remaining faithful and facing forward on the long journey to the Easter joy of resurrection. Chaucer said those pilgrims met in accidental companionship. I don't believe in those kinds of accidents.

Are We There Yet?

Grant, most merciful Lord, to your faithful people pardon and peace, that they may be cleansed from all their sins, and serve you with a quiet mind; through Jesus Christ our Lord, who lives and reigns with you and the Holy Spirit, one God, for ever and ever. **Amen**.

Lesser Feasts and Fasts

The Second Week in Lent

The Third Week in Lent
Insight and Inspiration

The angel of the LORD came a second time, touched [Elijah] and said to him, "Get up and eat, otherwise the journey will be too much for you." He got up, and ate and drank; then he went in the strength of that food forty days and forty nights to Horeb the mount of God. At that place he came to a cave and spent the night there.

Then the word of the LORD came to him, saying, "What are you doing here, Elijah?" He answered, "I have been very zealous for the LORD, the God of hosts; for the Israelites have forsaken your covenant, thrown down your altars, and killed your prophets with the sword. I alone am left, and they are seeking my life, to take it away."

He said, "Go out and stand on the mountain before the LORD, for the LORD is about to pass by." Now there was a great wind, so strong that it was splitting the mountains and breaking rocks in pieces before the LORD, but the LORD was not in the wind; and after the wind an earthquake, but the LORD was not in the earthquake; and after the earthquake a fire, but the LORD *was not in the fire; and after the fire a sound of sheer silence. When Elijah heard it, he wrapped his face in his mantle and went out and stood at the entrance of the cave. Then came the voice to him that said, "What are you doing here, Elijah?"*

1 Kings 19:7-13

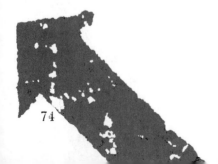

Are We There Yet?

The Journey

In the summer of 2015 at the age of 35, I traveled with a friend to the Galician region of Spain to walk the final 100 kilometers of *El Camino de Santiago,* also known as The Way of St. James. The *Camino* is an ancient pilgrimage with multiple routes, each winding toward a central point in the city of Santiago, where the shrine of St. James sits inside the Cathedral of Santiago de Compostela. Pictured on the left, I had dreamed of this pilgrimage since I first heard of its existence when I was sixteen. Due to multiple chronic illnesses that have increased my pain and decreased my energy each year, my own journey along the *Camino* felt like a now-or-never endeavor.   ***Teresa Pasquale Mateus***

Day 19

Teresa of Avila has been my patron saint my whole life. I was born on her feast day and named after her by the Grey Order nuns at my orphanage in Bogota, Colombia. I have been carried by Saint Teresa's energy (and sometimes her loud words speaking into my mind) through the hardest moments of my life. In truth, my pilgrimage to Santiago does not end in the pilgrim's city.

My pilgrimage moves beyond Galicia and westward into Avila, the city of my saint, my fiery mystic, on the 500-year anniversary of her sainthood. What moves me through every swollen toe, on blistered and bleeding feet, and every aching muscle moment of that 100-kilometer walk is the anticipation of the moment where I will see the walled Moorish city of my namesake.

I learn on the way to Santiago, and beyond in Avila, that what we think is the pilgrimage can often just be the whisper of our actual journey, beckoning us forward onto and into something that will transform us—a deep indwelling connection with God (and our saints) that is always there. In this moment of

Are We There Yet?

transformation, we find the eternal pilgrimage of our soul, regardless of the earth our soles tread. The walking is rough, but what I, along with many other pilgrims discover, is that life, our inner pain, and the search for the divine in our selves is the hardest journey of all.

The path to Santiago is blazed by shells and yellow arrows that illuminate the path through cities and hillsides, clearly defining which way to go. There is a sign along the pilgrim's road, about one day's walk out from Santiago, that simply asks, "What do we do when there are no more yellow arrows?"

The walking is hard but also simple. One foot, then the next; deep breath in and deep breath out. Soundtracks on iPods create a rhythm of steps and breath over each kilometer, each day, one at a time. The everyday, in-your-own-place journey— the heart's navigation of life's obstacles—is the much harder path to tread.

As the kilometers count down and the city draws near, I feel tension, anxiety, and a specific form of grief. The losses of the yellow arrows and the simple days of clear completions become acute. We mourn the ability to look back across the landscape of a day and see hillsides upon hillsides over which our feet have run and to say, "I did that. This is what I did today."

We walk like the prophet Elijah, pressing on through the pain, pushed forward by the whisper of spiritual motivation. Just as with our own experience, Elijah's journey does not truly begin until he reaches the end of his pilgrimage. There, he finds the breath and voice of God. It is in this moment that Elijah's pilgrimage manifests into more than a journey for journey's sake.

God asks Elijah the hard questions: Why? What is the purpose of his journey? What is he doing hiding on the holy mountain? Why has he come to this place?

For my heart, these are the essential questions of pilgrimage. We often can't even hear them, much less answer them, until the "pilgrimage" itself is at an end. When we hear these questions come, they serve as a reminder that what we think is the end is a beginning, and the beginning is an end—a circuitous cycle of life and death.

Just as Elijah hears the whisper of God in his ear, beckoning him toward the heart of God, I find myself in companionship with my patroness, Teresa of Avila, on my own journey. We will make it to Avila, and we will travel together. I call her into my pilgrimage from the start—she is my goal, my aim, my precipice of the holy cave at the end of the long road, the mystical void that I yearn to stare into and hear the voice of God whispering something into me that has been long-deadened by painful years.

Dearest God, we call to you to breathe with us, walk with us, and carry us forward on our pilgrimages into the heart of ourselves and into your own heart. Send us your guides to whisper into our lives, and help us find the way toward full love of and full embrace of you. **Amen.**

Are We There Yet?

Pilgrim's Journal
Suggested practices for the week

The pilgrim's path is one of rhythmic simplicity—the rhythm of steps and breath—just simply steps and breath. Commit to the rhythm of steps and breath in some way this week.

Take time away from devices and noise and find a place that can be your own pilgrim's path—a space where you can shut off and shut down everything but the rhythmic movement of your breaths and steps. Imagine them as the words of the prayer your heart needs to pray.

Let yourself go for a walk—but more than a walk. Let yourself leave behind everything that is obligatory and offer yourself a small daily pilgrimage in movement, in breath, in rhythm, and into inner quiet.

Day 20

On my fourth day of walking and still two days away from Santiago, my internal desire to walk into the pilgrim's city is in direct opposition to my body's screaming rage at the pain. I am in this predicament because of my own mistake of wearing new hiking boots for the weeklong trek (pro tip: Never, ever do that foolishness). I expected the pain of my endometriosis and fibromyalgia, but now my feet are torn up and bleeding. Naturally, this day includes long walks up and downhill, and my pack feels increasingly heavier despite the ritual unloading of unnecessary items each evening.

This particular afternoon, I am six hours into walking what will become my longest day of the pilgrimage. I walk up another endless, winding hill out of another village and find myself becoming angry and argumentative with Saint Teresa, trying to rationalize my way out of the situation. "I know the plan was to walk my way to Santiago, but I just want to get to Avila. Do I really need to finish this walk? Can't I just get a cab along this road right now? Okay, so this is the deal, if you really feel it is important for my process to continue on this road, just send me a single sign."

Almost the moment the thought utters itself into existence in my brain, two nuns in sandals appear seemingly out of nowhere and begin trekking their way up the hill at a steady pace, just ahead of me. "Okay, okay! I get it!" I mumble and grunt my way up the next stretch of hillside.

Sometimes the whisper of the divine shows up along the journey not how we expect it—and not how we want it—and beckons us forward. This beckoning to push onward is, in itself, an encounter with the divine.

Almighty and eternal God, so draw our hearts to you, so guide our minds, so fill our imaginations, so control our wills, that we may be wholly yours, utterly dedicated to you; and then use us, we pray you, as you will, and always to your glory and the welfare of your people; through our Lord and Savior Jesus Christ. **Amen**.

The Book of Common Prayer

Day 21

One of the critical elements on the *Camino*—or along any journey—is the baggage we carry. We come with our internal baggage in our hearts and our external baggage on our backs. Pilgrims learn very quickly that as we wrestle to walk with the internal weight of our feelings, we are also forced to address external weight, especially if we plan to make it all the way to Santiago, or Rome, or Jerusalem, or down the block.

As I walk the *Camino*, each night I go through a ritualistic process of purging and releasing that which I don't need to carry. This happens for almost every pilgrim on the path. Hostel floors and guesthouse common rooms are lined with the stuff we all brought but realize we don't need for the journey. There's so much we don't need for the journey but are convinced that we do! There's so much we can release, let go, throw away—extra stuff that doesn't serve us and weighs us down.

Into overfull garbage cans and donation piles go extra clothes, socks, and underwear. Extra soap, hair conditioners, and

Are We There Yet?

brushes are shared as offerings in communal bathrooms. In this way, all that we no longer need becomes part of a larger continuum of the ministry of hospitality—of meeting possible future needs of fellow future travelers.

Somehow the daily ritual reminder that we need so much less than we carry creates a way to release more than just our external excess baggage.

Soon the ritual of letting go moves from an outward exercise into an inward process—what the pilgrim's journey is really all about.

We all hit the road with too much baggage, deeply seeking the ability to let go, and hoping that once we arrive at the end of our trail, we will have a lighter load than when we started.

Dearest God, give us the strength to let go of that which we do not need for this journey of life. Help us to release from our lives, our hearts, and our spirits all that hurts us or is too heavy to carry. Help us release our burdens so that we might see you more clearly and hear you more crisply breathing light and life into our lives. **Amen.**

Day 22

I realize quickly on the pilgrim's path that I am unlikely to start and finish an entire day's journey with the same set of walkers. We cannot make a pilgrimage in a calculated tandem with another because pilgrimage never meets expectations—especially in relationship to our own rhythms and the rhythms of others. On the road, we may find ourselves alone; we are slower or faster than our companions, more sore and tired or more energized on a given day. Yet we also quickly learn that we are never really alone.

I begin to call this process "alone-together," meaning that while we are moving at our own pace, on our own path, we are also always doing it with others. Community on the *Camino* is everywhere, like a herd. We find the same people parking for the night in the same towns and leaving in some kind of synchronicity each day. We see familiar faces that we have passed or been passed by, and each night we gather in town or at the local hostels, greeting each other at the end of another long day.

We come to realize that while our own journeys and callings and paths may look and carry a different rhythm from others on the road, we are always in community and we can always find each other over and over again.

So, we travel alone; but even when we are alone, we are still together. There is something no longer lonely about that. This offers freedom to walk at our own pace and center our own journey, all the while knowing a beloved community is all around, waiting for us at the end of a long day, ready to share and hear the mysteries of our independent journeys.

Dearest God, offer us the courage to walk our own path at our own pace and to help us find the calling for our own journey. Let us also remember that beloved community surrounds us wherever we are, and let us know that even when we walk alone, we need not be lonely on this pilgrim path. **Amen.**

Day 23

Patron saints and ancestors are guides on the journeys we walk. For me, Teresa of Avila has been one of the strongest guides and companions along my life's journey. She has been with me from birth and has been calling me on a mystical path ever since.

I have always joked that I never had a choice about following a contemplative spiritual path; the decision was made for me before I could even cognitively know about it. I don't know—and don't want to know –what life might have looked like without her presence beside me.

Teresa's burning passion matches my own internal fire. Her ability to yell at me just when I need it, to get me in gear when I want to lie down and take a nap rather than press on, keeps me honest and fierce in my devotion.

On pilgrimage, I feel distinctly guided by her presence. We walk a beautiful, crowded path each day, full of magic, mystery, and the kind of deep grace that balances out pain and baggage and struggle.

Are We There Yet?

No matter where we journey, we need guides, spirits, ancestors, and beloveds who move with us, through us, and beckon us up hills we are too tired, angry, or broken to climb. We need to know—from the great beyond and out of time and from behind the veil—that this is possible. We need the whispers of those beyond this life to remind us of what we are truly capable on the hardest sections of our pilgrimage. Teresa is this for me on my *Camino*. Other beloveds who have passed have also visited me in hard places—my grandparents and other gracious saints. We all need guides to speak to our hearts, to prod and even yell at us, and to help us move along the path.

Dearest God and beloved saints, send your presence, light, and words into our lives in the hardest moments. Let us hear you. Let us listen. Let us welcome you in to walk by our side and carry us through our seeming breaking points, reminding us that we are capable of coming out the other side. **Amen.**

Day 24

Sometimes we need celebration. The night after the longest walk, after the nun sightings, and the motivational yelling of Teresa of Avila, I finally make it to the hostel. I have walked twenty-two kilometers that day, over four hillsides and through several towns. It is almost dusk on a steaming hot day…deliriously hot…mirage hot.

I am so exhausted that I pause less than a block from the *alburgue* because I need ten minutes to sit in the gratitude of having made it and with the painful exhaustion of what it has taken to get here.

I arrive at my destination for the evening, and a couple of travel companions are sitting and drinking wine. I drop my bag, fill a glass, and sink into the chair in front of me.

My longtime friend Marisol (pictured with me at the beginning of this chapter) and I stay up with the owner and other staff members, talking and laughing and drinking into the night. This time is a sweet reminder of the need for rest,

Are We There Yet?

for joy, and sometimes a little bit of recklessness to restore our spirits on the hard journeys.

We need to stop. We need to rest. We need to restore our souls with laughter and the joy of connection; otherwise none of the struggle serves a purpose. Life and pilgrimage cannot be all and only the hard parts. There has to be a reminder of what we are doing it for: love and life and light. We make this journey in relationship with others, finding new kindred spirits we never would have expected, meeting and connecting through smiles and beyond language, hearing hints of love and life as old as pilgrimage itself.

Dearest God, remind us to fill our cups with all that life has to offer and let us know we have permission to rest, to laugh, to find joy and love along the hard paths of life. Let us always hear you in the sound of happiness being crafted organically, in likely and unlikely places along our paths. **Amen.**

Day 25

When I arrive in Santiago, I feel relief in every possible way. My body sighs in every way a body can sigh. I think my toes even sigh. The pilgrimage itself ends at the base of the cathedral where daily, incense-laden liturgies occur and the names of pilgrims who completed their pilgrimage are announced.

I don't even make it inside the cathedral on this day; I drop all of my belongings on the cobblestones and let my whole body flop to the ground. I stare at the blue sky, skin sizzling in the hot, unencumbered sun, and I hear bagpipes coming from a nearby alleyway. I don't want to move ever again. I cannot believe I have made it. I didn't fall down—which for me, was a 90 percent or more probability—and I didn't give up.

I feel a new ownership and love for my body; I experience a profound sense of communion with this flesh and blood I have spent decades fighting. Pain and illness have clobbered my relationship with my physical self for so long. I hadn't realized how slowly pain had eroded my connection to my living flesh, my organs, my skin, and my muscles. I had spent so much of my professional energy and expertise talking about the inherent necessity of embodiment and connection and integration on the path toward healing, but I had not recognized this slow fading away of my own connection with my physical self. Something erupted on the *Camino*, maybe a survival reflex, and my emotional and spiritual self knew it could not make this particular journey without the agreement of my physical self.

At the end of the *Camino*, as I sit exhausted on the ground, I realize that my body has done this...and I have done this with my body. In the pilgrimage of life, it is necessary to see how we are connected to all the parts of ourselves. We cannot travel fully and completely without our whole self—mind, body, and spirit. We must feel our life and wake up to the experience of each and every step we take—feel it from our heels to our hair and through every fiber of our physical being. This connection and awareness wakes us up to life and to the fullness of the journey.

> *Dearest God, be with us in our whole self and speak into our lives through our bodies, minds, and spirits. Remind us to wake up to your presence and remember that we are embodied in our union with you and in our full selves when we feel our connection to the divine in every cell of our being. Let us celebrate our beingness in this embodiment and remember you are breathing life each and every day into our being.* **Amen.**

Fourth Week in Lent
Healing and Hope

In the first year of King Cyrus of Persia, in order that the word of the LORD by the mouth of Jeremiah might be accomplished, the LORD stirred up the spirit of King Cyrus of Persia so that he sent a herald throughout all his kingdom, and also in a written edict declared:

"Thus says King Cyrus of Persia: The LORD, the God of heaven, has given me all the kingdoms of the earth, and he has charged me to build him a house at Jerusalem in Judah. Any of those among you who are of his people—may their God be with them!—are now permitted to go up to Jerusalem in Judah, and rebuild the house of the LORD, the God of Israel—he is the God who is in Jerusalem; and let all survivors, in whatever place they reside, be assisted by the people of their place with silver and gold, with goods and with animals, besides freewill offerings for the house of God in Jerusalem."

The heads of the families of Judah and Benjamin, and the priests and the Levites—everyone whose spirit God had stirred—got ready to go up and rebuild the house of the LORD *in Jerusalem. All their neighbors aided them with silver vessels, with gold, with goods, with animals, and with valuable gifts, besides all that was freely offered.*

King Cyrus himself brought out the vessels of the house of the LORD *that Nebuchadnezzar had carried away from Jerusalem and placed in the house of his gods. King Cyrus of Persia had them released into the charge of Mithredath the treasurer, who counted them out to Sheshbazzar the prince of Judah. And his was the inventory: gold basins, thirty; silver basins, one thousand; knives, twenty-nine; gold bowls, thirty; other silver bowls, four hundred ten; other vessels, one thousand; the total of the gold and silver vessels was five thousand four hundred. All these Sheshbazzar brought up, when the exiles were brought up from Babylonia to Jerusalem.*

Ezra 1

Are We There Yet?

The Journey

My pilgrimage is a journey—a journey within, for sure, with an outward eye turned toward stewardship of our global home. I am nearly fifteen years out of prison, twenty-seven years without alcohol and other drugs (for the record, neither of which I believe are inherently bad; however, my inability to use them sparingly is). It has been thirty-one years since I took a human life, and almost fifty-four years since I came into being on this planet. And I am still searching.

I look within through meditation and self-inventory. I find further healing and salvation through all of God's creation: namely dogs, drunks, and trees. I push back against our collective entitlement as Americans to take everything we see, specifically our global home and its water.   ***Bo Cox***

Day 26

When I was approached to write for this Lenten devotional, I hesitated. I told the editor that I didn't feel very connected to Christianity these days. It seems to me that the religion named after Jesus has become more exclusive than inclusive. It feels like it's become more about prosperity and "what's in it for me" than brokenness and welcoming the stranger, feeding and clothing the poor, and visiting those in prison. Further, the church seems to be consciously (or subconsciously) tolerating a governmental system that leads the world in incarcerating its citizens. This, the editor said, was exactly why I needed to write. So I accepted the invitation.

I don't identify with mega-churches, prosperity theology, or a way of life that is more about what I get when I die than how I behave when I'm alive and how I treat those around me—especially those with less or those who don't look like me or believe like me.

I seek the sacred word of God—in the Bible, the Koran, the Torah, written on parchment paper, drawn in the sand, or heard in the wind through the trees, uttered by a robed official

Are We There Yet?

of the church, a sweat lodge leader, an imam, or a bedraggled patient at the psychiatric hospital where I work. Writer Anne Lamott says simply, "We can assume we have created God in our own image when it turns out that he hates the same people we do." I would add to that: "I can assume I have created God in my own image when I think I understand God."

Today's scripture from Ezra is about rebuilding the house of the Lord. The dictionary says rebuild means to build something again after it has been damaged or destroyed, and the authors of the Old Testament have a pretty concise idea about what this rebuilt structure should look like. I am not an authority on anything, certainly not rebuilding a temple. I do, however, have a little experience with rebuilding a broken human, along with an alternative understanding of the God who makes this possible.

What I know has little to do with wealth or material possessions but has much to do with vulnerability and accepting one's brokenness. My education into rebuilding a broken human has more to do with muddy feet than golden carpet, with stumbling, not surefootedness, with need rather than entitlement, with being left off the invitation list (and being let in anyway) instead of being on the VIP list to begin with. What I have learned is that rebuilding a temple in our hearts has more to do with bad coffee, hand-me down clothes, and honest souls in musty church basements than prime rib dinners at five-star restaurants where lobbyists and politicians make million-dollar deals to benefit the already-wealthy at the expense of those crushed by poverty. Rebuilding the temple in our hearts has more to do with social workers who toil on the brink of that same poverty than administrators looking to retire early with a full portfolio of stock options.

Ezra's lesson talks about the stockpile of wealth being a tower of material proof that God is good—and we are thankful. It also implies that wealth is a measure of favor and, therefore poverty must be anything but God-like.

The tower I see looks a lot more like a soup kitchen than a palace; it looks a lot more like crumpled sheets on a lopsided cot in a homeless shelter than starched sheets in a king-size suite in a luxury hotel. My tower looks more like a young forest of trees planted by people who will never see them reach maturity than a city block cleared for another million-dollar church where all the pretty people go to be told God wants them to have lots of money and fancy cars.

This week, we are not talking about a physical journey. This week will be about being still, about the journey within, about looking at ourselves in the mirror and seeing the image of God. I will share stories that illustrate God's promise that just because something looks this way today doesn't mean that the promise will always look that way. I want to talk about the difference between bad days when it feels like no one appreciates me and everything goes wrong, and good days when I am tearfully aware of how fortunate I am to be alive—and how this difference is simply my attitude and perspective. We will also talk about how it is not a coincidence that dog is God spelled backward.

Are We There Yet?

Pilgrim's Journal
Suggested practices for the week

If you're fortunate enough to live where there is clean water, I invite you to cup some in your hands and try to wrap your heart and mind around the fact that you're holding the stuff of life itself.

I invite you to take time to plant a tree for the benefit of those who come after us.

I invite you to take a walk and talk to strangers who don't look like you. Really talk, look in their eyes, and listen to what they say.

I invite you to spend time petting a dog (or cat...or other animal) and open your heart to a love you can't earn or deserve.

Finally, I invite you to get up every morning this week and pray, "Thank you," or, "Whatever," or both. Then, the rest of the day, I invite you to act as if you mean the prayer.

Thank you. Or: *Whatever.* **Amen.**

Day 27

Before she was named Hope, she was brought to the animal shelter by her owner. We don't know what prompted this, only that she was at a shelter where they euthanized owner-surrender animals within days. The day came when her cage number was on the kill list, and it looked as if her life would be over before she was even two years old.

My friend Brenda runs Dogs as Family, an Oklahoma City dog rescue that operates on the energy and love of its founder and several volunteers. They are more of a virtual rescue operation, as they don't have a centralized physical location—just the homes of Brenda and her foster team.

Brenda had shown up at the shelter to pick up another dog, not Hope. As she was talking to the shelter operator, Brenda heard about a beautiful golden retriever/Great Pyrenees mix that was supposed to have been put down earlier in the day, but for some reason, she had been overlooked. "If you want her, you better take her. They won't skip her again tomorrow."

Are We There Yet?

Brenda didn't even have a crate for this rescued animal, so she looped a spare piece of rope around the condemned dog's neck and led her from certain death to the safety of her van. On the way to town, Brenda phoned her team and found the dog a temporary foster home. Later that night, Brenda named the dog Hope.

That was almost three years ago. For the bulk of those three years, Hope has been at home with me and my wife, Debb. Hope and I are a certified therapy dog team, and she goes to work with me almost every day. When Hope isn't brightening the days of people at the psychiatric hospital, she is reminding Debb and me to be thankful for second chances—and four-legged angels.

Among many things, Hope teaches me that just because life looks one way at a certain time, it doesn't—and most likely won't—look like that forever.

Thank you. **Amen.**

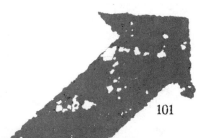

Day 28

Besides being able to take a therapy dog to work on a regular basis, one of my deepest joys is facilitating a guided-meditation group three times a week.

Sometimes folks in our group literally cannot sit still because of severe anxiety; others have been placed in our group because they were too disruptive in other settings—talking or responding to unseen-but-very-real internal stimuli.

Many participants in this group—including me—have avoided meditation with all the rigidity of those who think they already know "enough." Even so, we sit in a circle and practice finding the quiet beneath the noise in our heads, and beyond the visceral noise and tension of a state-run psychiatric hospital.

It's not like I accepted the invitation to start the meditation group with a willing heart. When I was asked, I hesitantly accepted, mostly because I wanted to bear some resemblance to a good employee. I figured it wouldn't take long to be a bust, and we could go back to something safe.

Are We There Yet?

Given the wide array of challenges faced by the people in our care, I knew no one would be interested in guided meditation—and if they were, they wouldn't be able to actually participate. But I would be a dutiful employee and try.

We are still going strong a year later. In fact, we have increased from one group a week to three. This has been a poignant reminder that I often don't know what's good for me.

Every session is powerful: We are in the most stressful and stress-filled place I have ever encountered (and I spent almost twenty years in prison), and yet at the end of our time together, we have created an atmosphere of peace. I often find myself with a lump in my throat at the nearness of something holy.

Left to my own devices, this is another gift I wouldn't have experienced.

Whatever. **Amen.**

Day 29

We just adopted another dog. Like Hope, he had been on the kill-list at a shelter.

I don't know why Tom-Tom ended up at the shelter. What I do know is that he's got "some issues." Most of the time, despite his high energy and loveable nature, Tom-Tom is noticeably scared. He sometimes flinches when I reach for something or make a sudden move. Tom-Tom likes to take all the toys he can gather to his area and not share with Hope. He also—occasionally and randomly—jumps, growls, and barks at people—though usually when they're on the opposite side of a gate or fence.

Of course, anyone who knows anything about behavior—animal or human—could surmise that this poor guy has been hit (or worse) at some point in his past. My wife Debb and I have committed to providing Tom-Tom a safe home where (hopefully) in time, he will come to believe that those painful experiences are in the past and will stay there.

Are We There Yet?

No matter how many times I tell Tom-Tom that he won't have to suffer any more abuse, I sometimes make things worse. When I'm loud or angry around him, his fears return and with them, his bad behaviors.

The only way I have managed to stay calm during one of his tirades is when I remember not to take it personally. I have a tendency to personalize his misbehavior when, for instance, he begins barking when a show *I want to watch* is on TV or when I'm in the middle of something *I want to do*.

This tendency—to personalize and become angry about behavior that interferes with *my* agenda—has plagued me most of my life. The only antidote I have found is for me to remove myself from the center of my universe and accept life on life's terms, not mine.

Whatever. **Amen.**

Day 30

✳

I have been out of prison for almost fifteen years. In that time, I've had the same employer (in fact, I'm nearing a time when I can retire). Debb and I bought a home. I have done things and been places that I never would have dreamed possible at one point in my life. Heck, I get to take a therapy dog to work with me!

Another thing I can do, if I choose, is hop in my car and drive wherever I want. That wasn't always the case. When I was in prison, Debb would occasionally talk with me about irritating traffic conditions. I would mention how I'd just like the opportunity to be out driving—and how that appreciation would soften any road rage I might experience.

You can imagine Debb's pleasure at being able to remind me of this when I cuss about someone in traffic. "Oh, I'd just love to be able to have the opportunity to drive," she'll say, pelting me with my own words. "Well, I didn't realize how many idiots are out here," is my usual response.

The truth is, Debb is right. When I am irritated to the point of anger, I have lost perspective. And, the thing is, *perspective is everything.*

These days, the only difference between a good day and a bad day is my perspective. This way of seeing the world has the power to change the gift that is my life into something to be endured or suffered through. Likewise, I have the ability to change what I think I'm enduring or suffering through into the gift that is my life.

Thank you. **Amen.**

Day 31

Not long after I went to prison, my dad told me about a pine tree he found growing out of a big rock, not far from the cattle guard in his driveway. He was struck by how the tree was growing in an environment with no noticeable sustenance. He found comfort in the tenacity of this tree and believed it was a sign that I, too, could grow in a less-than-fertile environment.

Over the course of the next seventeen years, I would hear about the progress of that tree—about how it continued to grow and how finally it even broke the rock it had been growing out of.

I understood the symbolism in this story, but not to the deepest degree until I stood beneath the huge pine with the split rock at its base. I look at it every time I visit Dad.

Somehow, I believe this lesson in tenacity and the will to live is connected to the pine trees I've planted on my own land. Scattered among the native hickory, oak, cedar, and numerous other trees are more than 100 pines—yellow pines, white pines, and Virginia pines.

Are We There Yet?

In much the same way that Dad's pine provided spiritual guidance—grow where you are—these trees continue to lead me. While the deciduous trees bloom, turn colors, and drop their leaves, the pine trees stay green. They remind me that there is nothing wrong with following your own path while others follow theirs.

When I stand underneath a thirty-foot pine that a decade earlier I held in the palm of my hand, I am reminded of what God can do if I will just put in a little work. It is always more than I can ask or imagine.

I won't be around when these trees are fully mature; someone else will benefit from them. And as I walk through the trees, I am reminded that I am at my best when I am not operating out of myself, for myself.

Thank you. **Amen.**

Day 32

On the backside of our property are a couple of gullies where years of torrential spring rains have cut deep and wide into the sandy soil. Even if it were rocky soil, water would shape these gullies the same way, just slower. Water, given enough time, can carve channels through solid rock.

For the past three decades, Oklahoma has averaged about fifty earthquakes a year. However, in 2015 the state recorded more than 900 seismic events. Scientists say the dramatic increase is because of the injection of water deep into the earth— water that has been contaminated during the extraction and production of oil and gas. This contaminated water, forced into the rock, causes the formations to shift and adjust for the added pressure and content.

Across the world, there are places where clean water is so scarce that people regularly die from lack of it. In the Christian tradition, water is used to baptize people into the faith. In both situations, water is life.

Are We There Yet?

In other places, all people have to do to access clean water is turn on a faucet. In many of those same places, ample water resources provide recreational opportunities. Multi-million dollar businesses are built in these locations with the assumption that there will always be plenty of water to play on and in and with.

In California, beginning in the late 1800s, people with money and power decided to turn the desert that was Los Angeles into an oasis. By deceit and force, they took water—most of it from a place called Owens Valley—and created a false and unsustainable ecosystem, destroying the valley and the surrounding areas.

In many places, greedy people have sucked the water from aquifers, nature's underground water tanks. Even if we shut off all the water wells today, it would take hundreds of years to replenish many of these aquifers.

Water is many things to many people. So too is God. Hopefully, we can all learn to view water in a more reverential manner and treat it like a gift, not a commodity. And hopefully we can do the same with God.

Thank you. **Amen.**

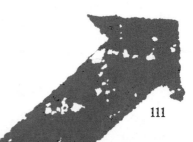

The Fifth Week in Lent
Community and Companionship

Soon afterwards [Jesus] went on through cities and villages, proclaiming and bringing the good news of the kingdom of God. The twelve were with him, as well as some women who had been cured of evil spirits and infirmities: Mary, called Magdalene, from whom seven demons had gone out, and Joanna, the wife of Herod's steward Chuza, and Susannah, and many others, who provided for them out of their resources.

Luke 8:1-3

The Journey

My disability does not stop me in my tracks. Nor does anything else. I sometimes travel across the country and even around the world. No matter where I go, God is always with me, leading and cheering me on. In this photo, I'm moving forward, along with several precious Honduran girls who wanted to imitate what they saw in me. They tried to "walk" the way I do! Each of these girls has her own personal journey, as I do. However, we walked this bit of it together, holding each other's hands and moving forward in courage and in hope.

Minda Cox

Are We There Yet?

Day 33

I am not yet thirty, but I have been on pilgrimage for all of those years. From the very beginning of my life, God has led, carried, sheltered, and defended me. God will also bring me to my journey's end, which is the same for all of us: fullness of life in God.

As a child, this was all hidden from me. Only much later could I see how carefully my path was laid and how well God has prepared me to travel along it.

God, who loves like a mother, grieved with my family in India as they sorrowed—aware the very day I was born without arms or legs that they could not take care of me. Together with my American family, they have walked, as God has made us able, into the embrace of God and into the complex world of adoption and reunion, of separation and unity.

God spoke in the minds of the doctors and nurses in the hospital where I was loved for seven months as a newborn and infant. During those months, much of my future personality was formed by their care for me, by their determination that

I be cherished and cared for, by their fierce insistence that I never be relegated to some back room.

God dwelt in the hearts of the social workers—those kind Hindu, Parsi, and Christian advocates who cared for me and so many other children separated from their first families, often unintentionally. Showered with real mother-love, disabled and able-bodied alike, many of us awaited new lives through adoption.

God's very presence lived within the adoption workers in Seattle as they carefully searched for a family willing to raise me as their own, despite my missing limbs. God carried me into the arms of my American mother and my four older sisters. Adoption too is part of my journey, and my pilgrimage.

God took me—and each of my adopted sisters—into arms of love and strode with us through oceans of laughter, along trails of tears, through valleys of doubt, and onto mountains of sunshine and triumph. My mother, too, felt insecure raising her motley crew and turned again and again to the God who led us into paths of ever-broadening freedom.

God still pushes me forward on my pilgrimage. Sometimes other adoptees talk with me, expressing hurt and anger over the loss of their first families. I have an opportunity to say that I share that loss with them. Like them, I wish I could have been raised in colorful, noisy, beautiful India. I wish I had grown up with my mother and father in the tiny village near Udupi.

But anger and resentment do not have to be part of my recovery from the grief of this loss. No one caused this loss. It just is. And there is joy and ordinary happiness in my life in spite of it. I am a person who was adopted—this is how I entered my American family. Adoption alone doesn't explain who I am, where I am going, or where I have been.

Even my disability, which is simply a part of who I am, doesn't define or describe me, either. It is real, but it is not the whole of my reality. As I have rolled my wheelchair with God alongside my family, I have slowly come to realize that my disability does not hinder me. My attitude might drag me down or hold me back—but not my missing limbs. This realization has become a great gift to me on my journey and has kept me from drowning in envy or discouragement.

As I go forward in faith, I speak to anyone who wants to listen. I write, paint, and draw. At first, art drew me to Beauty, who is God. I rested in this. Now it is Beauty I expect to see face-to-face one day: Beauty, Love, the Way, and Truth, and my Life—Jesus, Lord of all creation.

God leads me along all these many paths, each winding toward my goal, down gravel roads or up long driveways, to listen to elderly people, talk to discouraged moms and dads, and hang out with school children. Mostly, I tell them stories through my art and with my words. And I love hearing the stories they share with me in turn.

The stories we hear and the stories we tell encourage us to be vulnerable with each other and to push us forward in our journeys toward Jesus. They help us see where we've been and where we are going. Through stories, I have learned to walk, ride, run, and dance into a life that is abundant and free. And that is just part of my pilgrimage.

Your story matters. Your life is also going somewhere—toward God, however strange the pathway may seem to be. My life hasn't been written in straight lines; it isn't readable that way either. But I am pressing on, as I hope you are—not just on terrific days, but also through darker, difficult, and confusing ones. Whatever obstacles and places of discouragement present themselves, I remember the song from Sunday school: "I have decided to follow Jesus," as closely as I know how, "no turning back, no turning back."

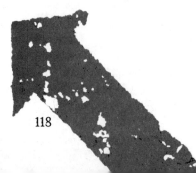

Are We There Yet?

Pilgrim's Journal
Suggested practices for the week

Try reading that simple Sunday School song—or sing it—every day this week: "I have decided to follow Jesus, no turning back, no turning back." Repeat the lines several times as a way to quiet your thoughts and still your soul.

Think about what a journey of following Jesus might look like in your everyday life.

Lord God our creator and constant companion, you walk with us from the time we are brought into this world; give us courage to follow you. We are created by the Love that lasts forever; teach us to love. You are the one whose hand we hold, and on whose shoulder we cry. Thank you for wiping each tear and sharing in every laugh. You grieve with us when we experience loss, and dance with us when we rejoice. May we continue to be vulnerable and simple, that we might be free to follow wherever you lead, and so to draw others nearer to you through our own journey. **Amen.**

Day 34

I am not adopted. My American mother adopted me. Adoption is how I entered my family. But I am not a label, or an event, or even a series of events.

Adoption is always complex. It is a result of loss, always. Birth mothers may forever grieve the loss of their child, no matter how that occurred, or why. Likewise there are adults who, even having grown up in good adoptive families, continue to suffer the loss of their first family. Adoption is intended to ameliorate those sometimes-inevitable losses. For me, it has.

I am the daughter of Kalavathi in India and Catherine in the United States. I have sisters here and I have sisters there. And I am content.

But more than this, I am Minda, who has a busy social life having lunches with friends and enjoying conversations over cups of coffee.

I am Minda, who delights in my nieces and nephews, in all kinds of music, and in good movies.

…who loves hours of quiet, who gains strength and receives energy from silence and solitude with my Lord.

…who loves rainstorms, waterfalls, rivers, and oceans; wind chimes, forests, woods, hills, and mountains; herbs, flowers, butterflies, and birds.

…who appreciates sunrises and is mesmerized by sunset and moonlight and lightning bugs.

…who loves to let watercolors sing as I paint and to watch stories flow from my computer screen as I write.

…who uses my voice to speak out for the abused and the disabled and against racism, violence, and injustice.

…who lives with a disability but who also simply goes about ordinary life just like you.

I am not disabled.

I am Minda and having been adopted—however important that is—reflects only part of my story and identity.

I am Minda, a follower of Jesus. And that is enough, more than enough, to carry me on this pilgrimage.

Beloved God, you have created each of us in your own image, and you are present with us as we discover the shape of our lives. Our stories are part of your own great story, and our identities are shaped by your love. Help us, protect us, remind us, and encourage us to embrace who we really are: your own beloved children; we pray this in the name of Jesus, your son, our Lord. **Amen.**

Day 35

You may be wondering exactly how I make my leg-less way on the journey God has set before me. The answer is that I mostly depend on my electric wheelchair.

That chair serves as feet that carry me to meetings, doctor's appointments, the grocery store, the art gallery, and to church on Sundays. If I drop something, it lowers so I can get onto the floor and retrieve the object. I can sit comfortably at any table height.

But on a warm summer night last June, my electric wheelchair completely ground to a halt. The actuator, which raises and lowers the seat, became utterly exhausted and finally put itself out of its misery. It died an undignified death with a series of horrific grinding noises. Nothing worked to revive it.

Fortunately, my chair collapsed at home. But I was stuck indefinitely—I couldn't go anywhere alone. I couldn't even get myself up to the table to draw or take myself to the refrigerator or shower. I needed help to do even the simplest things. And I didn't like this one bit.

Are We There Yet?

It seemed as if I was on a long "pause," that my hiking days were done. If you know what it's like to wrestle with insurance companies and coverage plans, you know this is a real fear. The struggle between Medicare, Medicaid, my physician, and the medical equipment company went on for over six months. The wheelchair had been repaired so many times and was so old that a new one was the only realistic solution. Meanwhile, my broken chair sat idle. Finally, my faithful mechanic came out to manually put the seat in one position, just so I could walk, even if I couldn't get up or down.

Eventually a new chair was approved, then ordered...then the order was corrected, and the chair was re-ordered. And finally, finally my new chair arrived.

God walks with me when it's easy; God also walks with me in inconvenient circumstances. And together we continue on, heart in heart, arm in arm, enjoying the journey.

O God of peace, you have taught us that in returning and rest we shall be saved, in quietness and confidence shall be our strength: By the might of your Spirit lift us, we pray, to your presence, where we may be still and know that you are God; through Jesus Christ our Lord. **Amen.**

The Book of Common Prayer

Day 36

I love the rain, and I savor the scent of it. I feel very close to God during a thunderstorm. Nevertheless, driving my wheelchair can sometimes create stress.

I was on my way to a meeting. I left the house a little earlier than usual because the sky was getting dark. I hoped to arrive at my meeting before the storm started. Alas, barely ten minutes into my walk, rain poured out of the sky, millions of droplets dancing in the twenty-mile-an-hour wind, soaking me completely.

My poor yellow poncho wanted so badly to be part of the fun—it kept blowing in my face and whipping around in the excitement. I kept trying to hang on to it for a little protection. Maybe I should have let it fly away since it was definitely not keeping me dry!

I finally reached a grocery store—the halfway point to my destination—and straggled inside. I was wet, shaken, and annoyed. The fact that my glasses were speckled to the point where I was practically blind did not help...that I

Are We There Yet?

have no hands with which to wipe them off was definitely a compounding insult to my irritation.

The friendly young woman at the service desk greeted me as if this were a wholly ordinary event—which, for me, it is! She gave me a cloth to wipe my face, glasses, and neck, and she brushed down and smoothed back my wind-blown, dripping hair. We found a new poncho, which she helped me put on. She even came up with the idea to tape it down to my chair, so that it would not fly around wildly and would keep me (mostly) dry. Her simple acts of kindness were rays of sunlight in my dark and stressful morning.

The meeting ended up going just fine—although everyone had gotten at least a little wet. We laughed, did our work, and enjoyed each other. There was no crisis, just inconvenience—and all of us shared that.

And my journey continues, unimpeded!

> *Dear God, you who are both mother and father to us,*
> *thank you for people who come alongside us and help us*
> *on our way. Remember their names, even if we do not.*
> *Bless them. And give us an open heart so that we can*
> *accept the kindness of strangers as well as friends. Help us*
> *to walk forward day by day with graciousness and trust.*
> *In Jesus' Name.* **Amen**.

Day 37

Our pilgrimage lessons include learning when to let some things go.

On a cool evening this spring, I became aware of a houseguest—or rather housepest—I had not noticed before. A mouse scurried out from behind the living room couch and into my room, taking noisy shelter behind my computer desk.

"Oh, if my niece Olivia were here, she would capture this creature in a matter of seconds," I grumbled. But it was late. Olivia wasn't coming. Mom was away. I was on my own with a mouse loose in my house.

I wasn't comfortable sleeping in my very low bed, listening to him chitter about. Finally, I made myself a bed on the couch, still unhappy about my housepest. I finally dozed off until around four that morning.

A loud, scratching noise woke me. I was rather annoyed at having been jolted from my slumber. That little mouse was becoming so obnoxious that he couldn't be ignored. By now,

Are We There Yet?

the mouse had traveled to my mom's room, despite her door being shut. Slowly I crept out of bed, walked into the room, switched on the light, and suddenly the noise stopped. I looked just in time to see him scramble under Mom's bed.

Recalling that mice love peanut butter, I got back in my wheelchair, made my way into the kitchen, and pulled out the jar. By that time, the mouse had returned to my room and hidden under the computer. I applied some peanut butter to a spatula and put it at one end of my desk. I watched and waited silently as my housepest slowly edged toward it. As I prepared to cover him with a net, he rushed back to Mom's room and back under her bed. There he stayed. Silent.

I gave up the chase and finally slept, too.

Olivia came the next morning, but the mouse was gone. I never saw or heard him again. How he managed to escape, I will never know. There are some battles we are not going to win. I would never have been successful in catching that mouse. Giving up, letting go, not fighting—often this is the best way to travel happily.

> *Spirit of God, our teacher, help us to understand and accept the realities of our lives, even when we discover that some circumstances will never change. Remind us in these difficult hours that we can trust you. Give us the power to relinquish anxiety, knowing that nothing happens outside your awareness and compassion, through Jesus Christ, our Lord.* **Amen.**

Day 38

Jesus speaks to his disciples, his enemies, his followers, and crowds of hangers-on every single day. He talks to religious leaders, women, foreigners, tax collectors, and children. And he speaks out about the things that bother him, too.

Jesus' words make him enemies among those we might expect to love him and friends among people we might otherwise ignore or despise. His words do that.

We need to listen to Jesus.

Jesus speaks to every generation, in every nation, under every circumstance, and in every situation. And to follow him, to walk alongside him, we need to be able to hear what his words mean for us in our present moments and daily lives.

I do not call myself a political person, but as I grow older, I find myself becoming more openly vocal in the cause of justice, for the sake of love—God's love.

I had never attended a rally before, but I had been asked to speak for this particular one, and I agreed. At the rally

Are We There Yet?

site, people waved rainbow flags, and children carried signs defending human rights. There was some anxiety fluttering around the crowd, but there was also happy laughter. On that sunny November afternoon, a large, peaceful crowd came together to stand as one for freedom and justice—for all of us.

We listened to presentations against racism, homophobia, sexism, environmental degradation, and police brutality. Cheers encouraged each speaker. Angry counter-protestors shouted obscenities. And I was nervous.

When my turn came, I rolled up to the microphone and shared my concerns about threats to Medicare, Social Security, and Medicaid, to physical and occupational therapies, special education opportunities for children with disabilities, and independent living opportunities and jobs for adults with disabilities. The crowd grew quiet, then enthusiastic. The more I spoke, the more urgent my words seemed to be. We were all there together—journeying, standing strong, loving each other. And the Spirit of God was in our midst.

Almighty God, you proclaim your truth in every age by many voices: Direct, in our time, we pray, those who speak where many listen, and write what many read; that they may do their part in making the heart of this people wise, its mind sound, and its will righteous; to the honor of Jesus Christ our Lord. **Amen.**

The Book of Common Prayer

Day 39

Our journeys to God are not supposed to be solemn at every turn. I truly believe God intends for us to have fun on the pilgrim roads of our lives. Our pilgrimages are full of adventure—a rich mix of pain and joy. God knows that some of the silly mistakes we make along the way deserve a good laugh. There are times when I wish someone were around to capture my most hilarious and ridiculous moves.

One sunny afternoon as I was making lunch, I found myself struggling with a plastic packet of soy sauce. For some odd reason, I wasn't able to rip it open with my teeth. The scissors had been shoved to the back of the silverware drawer, so I couldn't reach them. After a few minutes of frustration I decided to pull out one of Mom's sharpest knives, merely intending to make a small slit in the pouch so I could squeeze the liquid out.

The tip of that knife had a very different idea. Talk about an explosion…soy sauce sprang out of the package into my eye and proceeded to paint itself all over the stove and our white kitchen wall. I was stunned to see that there was nothing left for my chicken and rice stir-fry. Who knew there was so much sauce in such a tiny package?

I laughed so hard that both my sides hurt. I could just picture how this scene would look on *America's Funniest Home Videos*! As soon as I was able to pull myself together, I wiped up some of the mess. My elderly neighbor came to help me clean up the rest. After she left, I found some bottled soy sauce in the side door of the fridge.

I'm sure God was laughing with me that day. Rather than weeping because I struggled, God showed me how to turn the situation into a moment of pleasure and release. Besides, my dinner wasn't ruined! A sense of humor gives us the God-blessed ability to laugh at ourselves all along the way.

God, you give us the gift of laughter to delight and refresh us. It isn't always easy to laugh when we could get mad or resentful, but in laughter, we find you lifting our hearts and renewing our spirits. Teach us to relax and find the humor in our everyday lives, and let it bring us closer to you; through Jesus Christ our Lord. **Amen.**

Holy Week
Reconciliation, Redemption, and Returning Home

Do not let your hearts be troubled. Believe in God, believe also in me. In my Father's house there are many dwelling places. If it were not so, would I have told you that I go to prepare a place for you? And if I go and prepare a place for you, I will come again and will take you to myself, so that where I am, there you may be also. And you know the way to the place where I am going.

John 14:1-4

The Journey

Working as a newspaper writer (Victoria) and photographer (Frank), we found the work rewarding: We enjoyed writing and taking pictures. And yet Victoria found it increasingly difficult to call someone after a tragedy to ask how he or she felt about it. Frank grew troubled by the adrenaline rush of photographing news. One morning, Frank looked through the lens as the coroner opened the body bag, and a mother screamed as she saw her son. He didn't take the picture. Instead, we planned a hike of the Appalachian Trail (AT) to find ourselves anew.   ***Frank and Victoria Logue***

Day 40

When we set out to hike the 2,190-mile Appalachian Trail in a single hike, we wanted a spiritual journey, a time to reset, an opportunity to determine again what mattered most. No one told us that hiking does not afford a chance to think deep thoughts. Contemplate your place in the cosmos if you like, but you are likely to find that in doing so, you lose touch with your physical surroundings. In a moment, a hiker can trip over rocks or roots and end up face-planted into the trail, pressed down under the weight of a forty-pound pack. You must focus on the present while hiking.

Even with the lack of deep thoughts, the trail is beautiful and alluring, and the decision to hike the length of it greatly simplified our lives. For six months, our only concerns were the very basic requirements of survival—food, shelter, and water. Hiking the AT was quite simple in that we always knew the goal. Mapping out where to buy food and fuel for our stove took careful planning, but our basic activity list for any given day was pretty much set for half a year.

Weather remained the one obstacle around which we couldn't plan. Hikers can choose what time of year to hike certain sections of the trail. Day or weekend hikers can always cancel plans if the weather looks bad. Hiking for six months straight offers no such luxury.

In Virginia, we were saturated with eight consecutive days of heavy rains. Each day, we trudged through a downpour, sloshing down the trail in wet boots. One afternoon, the site we planned on using for the night was so inundated with water that the new downpour had nowhere to go. A puddle covered the flat area usually reserved for tents.

We hiked on and narrowly averted tragedy in crossing a rain-swelled creek. We both undid our pack belts in case we needed to ditch our gear. Frank made it across, but the force of the water knocked Victoria under the current when a rock rolled underfoot. She found solid footing and popped up long enough for Frank to grab her by the arm and pull her onto the bank. We both panted from the exertion but didn't say a word as we thought about whether she could have wrestled out of the shoulder straps once under the rushing water. After catching our breath, we refastened the hip belts on our packs and walked on.

On the eighth straight day of rain, Victoria wrote in her journal, "I never knew my feet could hurt so much." We set out into the rain that morning. Within minutes of beginning our hike, we were once again soaked. But an idea began to take hold. The AT passed along Skyline Drive, and we were to hike quite close to a lodge with rooms for rent. Forget the hope of heaven; we were hiking toward hot showers.

By the time we got to Big Meadows on Skyline Drive, it was getting dark. We were completely saturated. We walked into the local inn and were regarded with the kind of disdain usually reserved for someone who has just accidentally tracked dog poop into the foyer.

The manager at the desk asked us to take our packs outside before he would speak to us. When we made it to the desk—with all eyes in the lobby on the couple that looked and likely smelled like wet dogs, tails between their legs, hoping to suffer no further punishment—we learned that the rate for a simple room was too far out of our price range to even consider.

We attempted to purchase a hot drink and sit in the bar a minute, listening to the folk singer playing live music. But we were instructed that unless we were renting a room, we needed to leave. We walked out into the rain to hike the three-tenths of a mile back to the trail and then the 3.4 miles in the dark to reach a three-sided wood shelter. Becoming one with the trail made us outsiders at the inn.

A pilgrimage is, of course, a metaphoric as well as physical journey, which often leads to internal shifts as we gain a renewed perspective. Seeing ourselves as God sees us is never easy under the judgmental glare of others. Sometimes the best we can do is to stay in the moment and find the resilience to face what the day brings.

Pilgrim's Journal
Suggested practice for the week

As you walk the journey of Holy Week, tracing Jesus' journey to the cross and grave, take time to walk through a cemetery. While a Victorian era graveyard is ideal, any cemetery will do. Don't concern yourself with what you should think or feel, just walk among the markers of lives past.

Almighty and ever living God, you created humans from the fertile soil, and breathed life into our bodies, enlivening our souls: Grant that as we make this earthly pilgrimage, we remain grounded in your grace and love through Jesus Christ our Lord. **Amen.**

Monday of Holy Week

As summer wore on, many of the water sources we relied upon were drying up. Hiking fifteen to twenty miles a day, our bodies were burning through water faster than we could find it along the trail. On a blazing hot day in Massachusetts, we simply could not go any farther. Our canteens had only a tiny bit of warm water held in reserve, and our throats were dry. Our bodies were craving water.

In desperation, we got off the trail on a back road. There were no houses in sight, but after rounding two bends in the road, we saw a house with a water spigot by the garage door. Water! We quickened our pace.

Our sense of decorum kicked in as we neared the house. Politely, we went to the door and knocked, almost hoping no one would be home so that we could quickly get to the hose and drink our fill. A woman answered, looking a little puzzled to find two sweaty, smelly backpackers on her doorstep. Her husband joined her at the door as we explained our parched predicament. They escorted us into their kitchen—where they plied us with cold lemonade from the refrigerator and, quite unbelievably, warm cookies. We found ourselves in a most luxurious oasis. Before we left, the lady and her husband topped off our canteens with fresh water and added ice cubes to keep the water cold.

Thirteen years after we stumbled to their door, I phoned the woman that other hikers have come to know as the "Cookie Lady." She and her husband never forgot the couple who came to their doorstep in need of water. She told me, "You enjoyed the cookies so much that I try to keep fresh cookies around for other hikers." This couple was changed by our encounter with them, and they never took the comforts of their home for granted. By the time I phoned years later to say thank you, we too had been transformed by their hospitality.

Source of life, your Son Jesus offered the Samaritan woman the living water that becomes a spring of water gushing up to eternal life: Grant us the grace to proclaim the Good News in deed as well as word so that others may find that same life-giving water, through Jesus Christ our Lord. **Amen.**

Are We There Yet?

Tuesday of Holy Week

An unbroken succession of small, white paintbrush strokes are the thread that holds together the 2,190-mile Appalachian Trail from Georgia to Maine. Found mostly on trees, or sometimes on rocks or posts, these brush strokes are the only Google map available for hikers. The system of paint blazes seems like a great idea until you find yourself thigh deep in snow and every tree on the trail has been powder-coated with snow.

One night in early April, fifteen inches of snow fell as we slept in an old barn that served as an Appalachian Trail shelter. As we hiked into a bone-cold day, a hunting dog ran out from the remains of a movie set. The incomplete structure was built to look like a house when filmed from a distant mountaintop. The snow was usually calf deep, with occasional drifts that were thigh-deep for me and hip-deep for Victoria. With the random dog leading the way, I broke a trail through the snow as best I could with Victoria wading through behind me.

We couldn't see any markings, and occasionally we stopped to brush the snow off a likely tree. Sometimes we found the mark that assured us we were following the trail rather than wandering aimlessly in the southern Appalachians. Other times, we found nothing. Invariably though, the dog knew the path. Once, we found ourselves following a clear path visible as a dip in the snow, but the dog cut down hard to the left. At the tree break was a white paint blaze we would have missed. We rapidly lost elevation, passing below the snow line and into rain. The hunting dog, which had been running ahead and then hurrying back to us, making twice as many miles as we, went ahead of us one last time, never to return as we reached the highway through the valley.

Yes, there is a spiritual realm, but we encounter that realm through our bodies and through the real stuff of this world. An ordinary dog became an angel for us by leading us where we had to go.

Creator God, you made the cosmos, filled it with all creation, and called it good: Grant that as you speak through your creation, we have eyes to see and ears to hear your still, small voice, through your Son Jesus Christ; who lives and reigns with you, in the unity of the Holy Spirit. **Amen.**

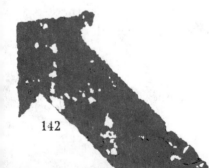

Are We There Yet?

Wednesday of Holy Week

As we hiked a relatively flat section of trail, Frank's right shoulder strap suddenly broke. The pack had been a state-of-the-art item when he bought it a decade earlier, with a plastic external frame designed to flex with a hiker's movements. But the plastic had degraded and the main crossbar cracked clean through. In short order, he duct-taped the crack and then pinned the bag to the bar at another point. We started hiking again only to have the pack virtually explode, multiple supports failing at once.

Hiking to a gravel road, we started walking back to town. Frank stood in the middle of the road, holding out his arms when a car chanced our way. The wary driver rolled down his window. Once he understood our problem, he drove us straight to a church-run hostel in Pearisburg, Virginia, which we had hiked through days earlier.

Frank opened the door of the hostel, slinging his ruined pack across the floor. One hiker asked, "Are y'all thru-hikers?" A second spoke up, "They might be thru-hikers, but I think they're through hiking!" He was right. How could we get to a place to buy a new pack—and if we did purchase one, how would the already-strained budget for the trip get us to Maine…and then back home?

As grace would have it, we found ourselves at the hostel in the midst of a group of hikers who had been hiking behind us steadily. They knew all about us and our hike—we had been writing entries in trail registers located at shelters along the trail. Soon, we were enjoying pizza and beer with friends who would not let us quit.

We called family. Victoria's dad bought us a new pack and along with her stepmother, drove to Pearisburg and took us back to the trail. In Vermont, we would seek out another hiker, part of this same group, and talk him into getting back on the trail after he decided to quit. Though we spent very little time actually hiking together, the group of us became stronger than any one of us.

Holy God, you exist in the Trinity of persons and out of love you created us to love you and to love our neighbors as ourselves: Grant that by your indwelling spirit we may be empowered to serve others as serving you, through the same Jesus Christ our Lord who lives and reigns with you, in the unity of the Holy Spirit, one God, now and for ever. **Amen.**

Maundy Thursday

Great slabs of granite loomed over us in the darkness, caught against the backdrop of a starry night. We paused to catch our breath—not from exertion, we were too excited to be tired—but from the depth of beauty that surrounded us. We turned off our flashlights. By the light of the moon and stars we could see peaks, lowlands, lakes, and the distant twinkling lights of Millinocket.

A week earlier, a group of us stopped at a shelter to enjoy a roaring fire as a storm raged. An idea that had occurred much earlier in the trip was once again suggested: Climb Katahdin—the northern-most peak on the AT—at night so we could be on the summit at dawn. We kept to the schedule and made it through the 100-mile wilderness to Abol Bridge. Only one other hiker kept the pact to join us in our late night hike.

We soared up Katahdin, the light from the crescent moon a beacon leading us to Baxter Peak. We passed by Thoreau Spring, marking the last mile to the summit, at 5 a.m. As we neared the top, we were forced to make a quick decision. A large cloud covered the summit of Baxter Peak. Did we want to remain where we were so that we could see the sun rise in the east, or did we finish in a cloud? We hiked on and as we did, the cloud—buffeted by wind above the summit—seemed to explode from the center and stream away in all directions. Silhouetted against the pale orange and yellow of the not-yet-risen sun was the sign that marked the northern terminus of the Appalachian Trail.

We placed the small stones we had carried with us all the way from Springer Mountain on top of the cairn that marked the end of the trail. Sobs of joy caught in our throats, and tears stung our eyes as shouts of exultation burst from deep within us. The sun painted the sky and then lit with golden rays the many ponds dotting western Maine.

O God, the heavens declare your glory as each day you renew the face of the earth with the light of your presence: Grant that as the darkness of this life seeks to envelop us, that in your light we may see Light, your Son Jesus Christ our Lord, who lives and reigns with you and the Holy Spirit, one God, for ever and ever. **Amen.**

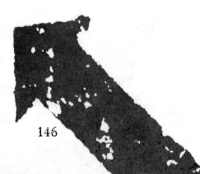

Are We There Yet?

Good Friday

The pregnancy was planned. We wanted to begin our new life as parents. And for five and a half months, we nurtured that dream even as all was clearly not right with the pregnancy. Victoria's doctor wanted to know exactly where the baby had been conceived. He had hiked the Appalachian Trail in sections, and he had done a little math and had guesses of his own. He seemed oddly disappointed when we said we were sure it was at the campground near Abol Bridge in Maine.

Years later, this doctor would get back in touch with us to let us know about some research he had read. While Victoria was in great shape by some measures, we had also spent six months starved for calories and eating a rather limited diet high in carbohydrates and too limited in proteins and essential vitamins to support a healthy pregnancy. The baby died having never been born; surgery was required, as was dealing with the pain of what was not to be.

Many years later, we would come to see how this loss marked our lives when our daughter—born two years later—spoke of her older brother who died unborn. She had heard us say that we never did come up with a possible girl's name. Our daughter felt the loss of her brother William through our grief.

The AT gave us a new life, even as we mourned the death of a baby who was not to be. We left newspaper work to forge our own path. Paid for by demanding and unsatisfying work in publications, we funded the writing of a first book and then began freelance writing and photography. We discovered a lasting purpose through relationship with Jesus.

Frank went on to finish seminary, and Victoria became a Franciscan tertiary, keeping a rule of life with others in the Third Order Saint Francis founded while living in the world. Together—with our daughter—we planted a new church in Georgia.

The redemption we found was not the life we hoped for when we ended the trail. What we found was so much more than we could have asked for or imagined.

Eternal God, you come to us not only in our hopes, but also in our suffering: Grant us the courage to seek you in joy and to bear the sorrows of others, strengthened by our Savior Jesus Christ who entered not into glory before he was faithful unto death on the cross; who lives and reigns with you and the Holy Spirit, one God, now and for ever. **Amen.**

Holy Saturday

We returned to Katahdin the fall after we completed the trail. Though so much of the AT had been a trip for just the two of us, we came to depend on the community of the trail. We longed to climb the peak with a group. This second time around, we would be part of a group. The only problem: This was not our group. The trip would be led by a hiker we had met briefly as we were hiking opposite directions. In many ways, our opposing directions had been a metaphor. He led a hiking group we had joined, and we were becoming the oil to match his water as we tried to mix. The trip offered enough of a lure to attempt it with strangers, rather than our old gang from the first time.

While lacking the poignancy of completing a six-month journey, we encountered more than we expected. The smell of the balsam fir trees at the base of the mountain connected deep in the wiring of our brains. Smells do this like no other sense can. We had been back to the trail in the South, but this scent was something we had been away from for nearly a year. The smell was—in a way impossible to put into words—home.

We climbed in daylight this time, able to see the boulders we had navigated by starlight on our first summiting trip. At Thoreau Spring, named for Henry David who hiked no farther, we encouraged less-experienced hikers to find the reserves for the hike to the summit. Thoreau was turned back by bad weather, but this day was a brisk fall day, perfect for the climb.

Back at the wooden sign marking the northern end of the trail, we were surrounded by a group of strangers who we were bonding with on the trip. Though it had seemed wrong when we signed on, the trip was just right.

Reconnecting to Katahdin with that group brought us back home in a way the bus trip back to Georgia a year prior could not. The journey was home.

O gracious God whose Son Jesus Christ had nowhere to lay his head, stay with us in the journey of this life as we seek your face in those we meet and grant us so to follow where you have led the way that we may find our rest in your eternal changelessness; through Jesus Christ our Lord, who lives and reigns with you and the Holy Spirit, one God, now and for ever. **Amen.**

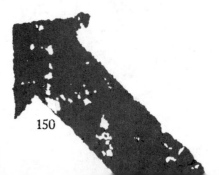

Are We There Yet?

Easter Day
Wonder

Then one of the seven angels who had the seven bowls full of the seven last plagues came and said to me, "Come, I will show you the bride, the wife of the Lamb." And in the spirit he carried me away to a great, high mountain and showed me the holy city Jerusalem coming down out of heaven from God. It has the glory of God and radiance like a very rare jewel, like jasper, clear as crystal. It has a great, high wall with twelve gates, and at the gates twelve angels, and on the gates are inscribed the names of the twelve tribes of the Israelites; on the east three gates, on the north three gates, on the south three gates, and on the west three gates. And the wall of the city has twelve foundations, and on them are the twelve names of the twelve apostles of the Lamb.

I saw no temple in the city, for its temple is the Lord God the Almighty and the Lamb. And the city has no need of sun or moon to shine on it, for the glory of God is its light, and its lamp is the Lamb. The nations will walk by its light, and the kings of the earth will bring their glory into it. Its gates will never be shut by day—and there will be no night there. People will bring into it the glory and the honor of the nations.

Revelation 21:9-14, 22-26

Easter Day

A pilgrim is on a quest for the sacred, a person with one foot planted in the kingdom of roots and another foot planted in the kingdom of motion. A tourist studies guide books and maps and wanders around an ancient abbey or a medieval monastery admiring the stained glass or the stonework. A pilgrim longs for the stones to speak and punctuates the visit with prayer, contemplation, and whenever possible, Holy Eucharist. The pilgrim stops, rests, and allots time for the soul to catch up.

Esther de Waal writes in the foreword to *Glendalough: A Celtic Pilgrimage*: "A holy place carries power. To be on pilgrimage is to move into a world where the dividing line between past and present, between this world and the next, between what we call sacred and what we call secular, dissolves. The outward journey is also a journey inward. We need to be prepared to let go of the accustomed patterns and controls that we impose on our daily lives, and instead be ready to be opened to what lives beyond—and what is most often expressed in symbol, image and poetry."

Are We There Yet?

As pilgrims we forget the office, forget the traffic, forget the stress and the ceaseless demands made by everyday life—we step away. We step away from busyness of life and seek time for reflection and discernment. Pilgrimage provides pilgrims not with an escape from their problems and issues but with an opportunity to walk through the issues that weigh heaviest on their minds.

The early Church Father Irenaeus wrote, "The glory of God is a human person fully alive." To be a pilgrim is to make a journey in search of what it means to be fully alive. On this Easter Day, we celebrate the the glory of God in the fully alive Christ, knowing that we never travel alone, that what seems like a dead end is really a new beginning, and all is truly well.

Marek Zabriskie

Grant us, O Lord, a pilgrim's heart and a pilgrim's spirit. May we step away from the ordinary and accept your invitation to set out on a journey, retracing the footsteps of pilgrims who have gone before us. May we experience you as we enter a way of simple living, as we pray with our feet and our hearts and as we encounter surprises along the journey. May we break bread with new companions, entertain angels unexpectedly, be beneficiaries of graceful hospitality, and discover you in each valley and watershed, field and forest, river and stream, in prisons and churches, in art and in laughter, sensing your presence and love in all things. May depth, not distance, be the goal of our journey, and may we come fully alive as we walk the holy way with you. **Amen.**

About the Authors

Bo Cox leads therapeutic activities at a psychiatric hospital and serves as a consultant to Saint Alban's School in Washington, D.C. He and his wife live near Norman, Oklahoma, with their beloved dogs. Bo has been writing for Forward Movement for more than two decades, both in *Forward Day by Day* and in several collections of meditations, including *I Will, With God's Help*.

Minda Cox is an artist, author, international missionary, and lifelong Episcopalian. A graduate of Southwestern Baptist University, Minda lives in Bolivar, Missouri, and is an advocate for other disabled people. Minda has written for *Forward Day by Day* as well as *For the Beauty of the Earth: Daily Devotions Exploring Creation*.

Nancy Hopkins-Greene is an Episcopal priest and serves at Church of the Redeemer in Cincinnati, Ohio. She is the author of *Moving Meditations* and has written for *Forward Day by Day*.

FRANK AND VICTORIA LOGUE are each well-seasoned authors with their own deep roster of articles, books, and published photographs—in addition to co-authoring several titles on hiking. They also have extensive experience hosting spiritual retreats. Avid and adventurous hikers, trails form a backbone for their writing and relationships. Frank serves as canon to the ordinary in the Episcopal Diocese of Georgia, and Victoria is a tertiary in the Third Order of Saint Francis. They make their home in Georgia.

TERESA PASQUALE MATEUS is a graduate of New York University School of Clinical Social Work and the executive director of The Mystic Soul Project. The author of several books on trauma and recovery, Teresa also contributed to Forward Movement's book, *Ashes and the Phoenix: Meditations for the Season of Lent.*

CATHERINE MEEKS is the retired Clara Carter Acree Distinguished Professor of Socio-Cultural Studies at Wesleyan College and serves as a lay teacher and advocate in the Episcopal Diocese of Atlanta. She is the chair for the Beloved Community: Commission for Dismantling Racism. She has led pilgrimages to historic lynching sites in the Episcopal Diocese of Atlanta, in addition to offering many continuing education opportunities for clergy and lay people throughout the Episcopal Church.

Are We There Yet?

Jeffrey Queen is an Episcopal priest and the rector of St. Andrew's Episcopal Church in Fort Thomas, Kentucky. He has served as chaplain to the pilgrimage to the American Proto-Shrine of Our Lady of Walsingham. He lives with his wife and two children in Northern Kentucky.

Marek Zabriskie is the founder and director of the Center for Biblical Studies, which promotes The Bible Challenge. Currently, more than half a million Christians in almost 3,000 churches have participated in this program. He is the editor of several *Bible Challenge* books published by Forward Movement, most recently *A Journey through Acts* and *The Social Justice Bible Challenge*.

About Forward Movement

Forward Movement's mission is to help you grow as a follower of Jesus Christ, and to support you in your spiritual journey. We are committed to inspiring disciples and empowering evangelists. Forward Movement produces many valuable resources, just like this book you're holding. But we are a ministry, not a publishing company.

We live out this ministry through offering books, daily devotional materials, studies and curriculum for small groups, apps, websites, and and online resources. More than half a million people read our daily devotional resource *Forward Day by Day*, which is also available in Spanish (*Adelante Dia a Dia*) and Braille, online, as a podcast, and in an app for smartphones and tablets. We mail copies of *Forward Day by Day* to readers in more than fifty countries, and we donate nearly 30,000 copies a quarter to prisons, hospitals, nursing homes, and to those serving in the armed forces.

We are actively seeking partners across the church and additional ways to provide inspiring and challenging resources to our brothers and sisters.

Forward Movement has been a ministry of the Episcopal Church for almost 90 years, committed to living into our call as a ministry sustained by the sales of our resources and the generosity of our donors. Please join us in this ministry by visiting www.forwardmovement.org and make a donation or purchase a resource for yourself or a loved one today.

We are delighted to be doing the work of sharing the Good News of God in Christ, and we invite your prayers, support, and participation with us.

160   Are We There Yet?